DIRECTORY OF EXECUTIVE TEMPORARY PLACEMENT FIRMS

KENNEDY PUBLICATIONS

Compiled and published by Kennedy Publications, publisher of *Executive Recruiter News*, the confidential newsletter of the executive recruiting profession.

Templeton Road, Fitzwilliam, NH 03447

(603) 585-6544

ISBN # 0-916654-96-6

Price: $19

Table of Contents

Introduction 1

Resources 7

Some Pros and Cons 8

Firm Listings 9

Geographical Listing 29

Specialty Listing 33

More Growth in Small Field of Exec Temp 'Head-Renting'

What's the word on executive temporary placement? More.

More acceptance of the value of interim execs is driving the market past the education mode to widespread general use of exec temps.

More recruiting firms are adding the placement of exec temps to their array of services. Some see an opportunity to increase business by broadening services; others are simply responding to occasional client requests.

More executives, middle to upper management level, are pursuing exec temp placement work through interim exec placement firms and personal networking. For today's corporate executives, the reduction in job security has resulted in more interest in the challenges and rewards of temporary work.

More companies, downsized to the max, need interim execs for caretaker management (to cover open positions, some due to the Family Leave Act), restructuring, mentoring, and, perhaps the biggest area, for special projects. Hiring interim executives is no longer a sign of a firm's instability.

Overall, temporary workers number 1.6 million daily or 1.4% of the total U.S. workforce of about 118 million, according to the National Association of Temporary Services. Of the total annual payroll for temp workers of $19.6 billion, NATS says 5.2% is in the "professional" category and an additional 12% is in the "technical" area. In other words, professional-level temps — an admittedly ill-defined term — are earning more than $1 billion a year in total. If placement firms are involved in one-third of those placements, they are generating about $100 million in fees.

In this report, our seventh update since 1990, we identify 205 firms in the field, including 189 in the U.S. The largest of these, IMCOR, will have revenues of about $8 million this year; but for many firms on our list, exec temp placement is a small part of their service offering, so a total U.S. market estimate of $100 million also seems reasonable from that perspective.

What's the growth rate? The market is too young to measure well, but the 400% increase over four years in the number of firms we identify gives some indication. Our research also shows that most firms entering exec temp placement in the past four years have stayed with it, and people inside and outside the field agree it appears to be a long-term growth market.

Still, we emphasize: A $100 million market for placement of exec temps is only a tiny fraction of the $3-plus billion permanent search market here.

Shift to temps seems permanent

Today's corporate environment of downsizing, rightsizing, restructuring, family leave legislation, and special projects creates ideal circumstances for the employment of executive temporaries. And increasingly, it appears these conditions reflect a permanent change in the job market, fueling an ongoing demand for exec temps. The need for special expertise or for a fill-in during a search, the desire to "try out" a candidate, the lack of succession planning and a new tendency to keep company payrolls lean by chronic slight understaffing as well as post-recession economics all contribute to market demand.

Standing ready to meet the demand are a variety of exec temp placement firms that are successful because they perform an important screening function, quickly presenting the truly qualified from thousands of available job-seekers. Their biggest competition comes from the candidates themselves, who identify opportunities by networking. A recent survey of interim executive candidates by IMCOR found 48% were seeking work through personal networking.

Much media attention

The employment of executive temporaries has attracted attention far greater than the size of the market seems to justify. This may be true in part because exec temps are seen as symbolizing a larger overall shift in the complexion of the job market. Publicity has led to greater understanding and acceptance of the concept of employing interim executives, and therefore enhanced the market. Books such as *The Temp Track* by Peggy O'Connell Justice, *The Age of Paradox* by Charles Handy and, soon to be published, *The Portable Executive* by IMCOR Chairman John Thompson (see Resources, page 7) cite the emergence of the executive temporary market in their focus on redefining career paths.

Media attention also accounts for the flood of resumes sent to interim exec placement firms by the enormous number of highly qualified, available executives. Although there is certainly more talk than action, it seems clear that a fundamental change has occurred in corporate culture, employment practices and management structures and the strategic use of interim execs is an increasingly significant and permanent response to that change.

What's in a Name?

People who become executive temporaries are known by many names: interim executive, interim manager, flexible executive or flexecutive, contract executive, short-term executive, contract professional, line consultant, migrant manager, itinerant manager, company doctor, portfolio executive and even business commando, troubadour executive and throwaway executive. In a verbal reflection of today's corporate climate, many are "discouraged workers" (resigned to never getting another permanent position) in a "disposable job" created to accommodate new "accordion management." Corporate cultural changes and fallout from the recession may well have created a new "portfolio career" path well suited to the interim executive market.

(In an odd, related development, the firm Interim, which holds a federally registered trademark, is objecting to the use of the word "Interim" as a trade name, service mark or trademark. A service mark identifies some particular services or origin of services.)

These talented folks are recycled retirees, job hunters, golden parachuters, lifestyle seekers or refugees from the corporate routine, managers-turned-mothers and career interim executives. They are in between projects, unemployed or self-employed. They are pre-screened high-level professionals often earning more than $100,000 who are no longer saddled with a stigma about temporary work.

In fact, they prefer it. Many have become disillusioned by the evaporation of job security, are cautious about long-term commitments and are just as happy free-lancing or in a trial-marriage mode.

Candidates over age 55, who may have difficulty finding permanent posts, are, with their wealth of experience and expertise, ideal for exec temp placement. As the demand for mentoring increases, their skills will increase in value.

Working as an interim executive sounds appealing, but candidates must be realistic: out of databases numbering in the thousands per firm, placements per firm are often only in the single numbers per month. Searches must identify candidates with extremely specific talents and experience. Despite a growing market, with more market niches being covered, the chance of being placed as an interim exec is very slim indeed.

Interim executives who are placed are often overqualified for the jobs they perform. Their depth of experience and knowledge lead to shortened gear-up time. Current hot industries include manufacturing, healthcare, hi-tech and financial services, where job functions in marketing and business development — as well as the alphabet jobs of CEO, COO and CFO — are in demand. Most often, interim execs are brought in on the revenue-generating side. When brought in on the staff side, it is often to establish a function and then to turn it over to a lower level placement.

How the process works
An exec temp placement firm's typical fee is 20-35% of compensation.

Assignments average six months, although many are now running longer than planned due to either a poor initial job estimate or the performance of additional tasks by the interim exec while he or she is there. Many exec temp placement firms are now charging a retainer to start their search (one firm charges 10% of the yearly base salary).

The retainer helps protect the placement firms from the inherent cut-throat nature of the business, in which placement firms compete against time, each other, other methods of filling the jobs and the changing nature of these kinds of openings. Without the retainer, few assignments are exclusive, and the situation can simply go away.

The hiring corporation can treat the executive temporary as an employee, as an employee of the placement firm or as an independent contractor. Independent contractor status and determination of the employer of record should be carefully evaluated. The IRS now has a computer program designed to catch independent contractors who don't fit rigid criteria. Due to the crackdown on 1099 status, some companies are reluctant to bring in independents and are opting for an exec temp placement firm which provides insurance coverage and pays the taxes.

Placement firms that provide payroll and benefits services usually rely on an outside funding company to bridge the gap between payment of the employee and reimbursement by the client. Some companies also assume employer-of-record status and handle much of the ensuing paperwork.

One funding company, TriCom (John Leopold, 414-359-4343), currently funds 11 interim exec placement firms as well as support-staff temp placement firms nationwide. TriCom charges 5% of gross billings and handles funding, invoicing (using placement-firm stationery with funding company address), payroll processing, taxes and remittance of the net gross profit (in about 35 days) to the placement firm.

Who's making the placements?
Interim executive placement (a.k.a. flexible recruiting, management contracting, alternative, just-in-time or stop-gap staffing) is being offered by firms large and small, in the U.S. and overseas. Many permanent search firms are adding executive temporary placement. And, since many interim execs go permanent (at least 15% and as high as 75-80% for one firm we queried), search firms can get a foot in the door with a temp placement fee and then collect an adjusted full fee if the executive is hired permanently.

Firms take different approaches to offering an executive temp placement service. Some consider themselves purists; they see the placement of exec temps as a separate business from permanent search placement. Many permanent exec search firms view exec temp placement as an added service for which they are particularly qualified. (An increase in exec temp placement can often signal the onset of an increase in permanent placements as companies attempt to redress layoffs that ran too deep.) Yet other firms blend executive temporary placement with varying combinations of permanent search, management consulting and outplacement as a package response to a client's wide-ranging needs.

Merit Resource Group started five years ago to provide HR interim management and payroll services. The firm now places more than 200 exec temps per year for a client base of about 260 companies. But due to client needs, Merit's consulting practice has grown to become nearly as large as its temp placement service. Other firms have added a permanent search service to their interim placement offerings!

In many cases, selling both permanent and temporary placement may feel like a philosophical tightrope. To clients for whom search firms attempt to justify several-month-long searches and $50,000 fees, they are also saying that, on the other hand, they could find an exec temp in a few days for a relative pittance.

Large firms that supply temporary clerical help are inching toward exec temp placement by offering to fill gradually higher level jobs through their service networks. If this trend accelerates, it could become significant. After all, temp giant Manpower is now the nation's biggest private employer, with about 600,000 people on its payroll.

Around the world

Several large retained search firms now offer exec temp placement in Europe, where evolution of the EEC and strict employment laws requiring job security for permanently placed executives have boosted the demand for interim execs in many countries. But Europe is still a disparate place. The U.K. has an active exec temp placement market growing at an estimated 20 percent per year. Holland, which has very restrictive labor laws that fuel the use of temps, may have the strongest exec temp placement market in Europe. But Spain, for example, has labor laws that seem to hamper use of temps.

The placement of exec temps in Eastern Europe has been below expectations; and, because everything moves slowly there, exec temp engagements tend to run two or three years rather than the six or ninth months that is more typical in the West.

New Zealand and Australia are slowly increasing their use of exec temps and (perhaps coinciding with recessionary economic conditions similar to those that promoted growth in the U.S.) exec temp placement has begun to take off in Japan.

Interim executive placement is often referred to in the United Kingdom as "executive leasing," but should not be confused with "executive leasing" in the U.S. (the outsourcing of staffing and payroll functions). The U.K. market for exec temps is mature and growing as the economy improves there. U.K. placement firms often have 15 to 40 jobs going at any one time, and they generate an estimated $10 to $15 million in annual fees.

Search firms enter market

Of the large executive search firms, the biggest player in interim executive placement in Europe is Egon Zehnder International, through a joint venture called Executive Interim Management (co-owners are Boer & Croon Group management consultants and Euroventures investment group). EIM originated in Holland in 1978 and now has offices in Belgium, Germany, France, Switzerland, the U.K. and Australia.

New to the exec temp placement market are two more prominent European search firms: Norman Broadbent International, which offers the service through its affiliate NB Selection, and Mulder & Partner/Amrop International, which recently launched Mulder & Partner Interim Management.

Protem, a London division of Heidrick & Struggles, makes two to three interim exec placements per month working from both the Protem and Heidrick & Struggles data bases of candidates. As the recession abates, Protem's clients want fewer "company doctors" and more interims before they are ready to hire full-time. Only 5 percent of Protem's interim execs go permanent, but not because of client reluctance — it takes a lot to entice these well-paid, over-qualified execs.

Boyden International Ltd. offers exec temp placement upon client request in Europe but doesn't view it as a core business. Although Boyden's permanent search practice is growing, there are no plans to expand exec temp placement.

Korn/Ferry International, the world's largest search firm, entered the exec temp placement market in 1991 but closed the practice in 1992 after difficulties with its venture partner. There are no current plans to resume.

Alliances and associations
Alliances to facilitate cross-border work and associations to link interim executive placement firms with each other or with other service providers are cropping up on both sides of the Atlantic. Although many alliances are not yet highly active, the increase in this activity is another sign of the confidence in interim executive placement as a permanent growth market and a new and accepted standard in the corporate environment. A number of firms are positioning themselves now for future growth.

London-based Albemarle Consultants and interim management firms in France, Italy and the Netherlands recently created the International Interim Group. With success, the alliance may spread to Germany and Spain.

In mid-'93, IMCOR formed an alliance with Canadian-based KPMG Peat Marwick Stevenson & Kellogg. So far, activity is low, but hopes are high and IMCOR expects to formalize a similar mechanism for Europe within two years.

The Douglas Reiter Co. formed a strategic alliance with IntraManagement of Zurich to provide mutual assistance and provide clients with on-site assistance. As with other alliances, partners view this as a long-term play with a future advantage derived from structures designed now.

Ten exec temp placement firms in the U.K. have formed a professional association: The Association of Temporary and Interim Executive Services, whose members are bound by a code of ethics that addresses professionalism, confidentiality, promotional activities, competition, employment law, equal opportunity and resolution of disputes (see Resources, page 7).

So far, there's no association in the U.S., but Bill Coleman of Flynn, Hannock in Connecticut is interested in helping to form one.

Flynn, Hannock recently forged a link with GMS Consultancy Ltd. in Dunstable, England, to trade assignments and make referrals as needs arise.

Some notable firms
Perhaps the premier firm in the field of executive temporary placement in the U.S. is Interim Management Corp. (IMCOR), started in 1988 by John Thompson, former chairman and CEO of KMG Main Hurdman and executive vice chairman of Peat Marwick Main. After those firms merged, Thompson saw a need and an opportunity to place interim executives. His vision has been rewarded as IMCOR's revenues doubled yearly, now estimated at $8 million. IMCOR has offices in Stamford, New York, Chicago, Dallas, Rochester and Los Angeles. IMCOR places 200 interim executives per year (40% go permanent) and says business has never been better. IMCOR maintains a database of 15,000 candidates (only 50% are available at any one time).

IMCOR launched PROCOR, a professional services division, in November 1993. PROCOR, based in New York, supplies 4-to-5 temporary execs per month ($85,000 average) in accounting and financial services. PROCOR will soon add HR placement and expand from there. IMCOR's goal is to have the PROCOR service available in every IMCOR office.

Big news in exec temp placement is the launch of InterExec temp placement services by Management Recruiters International, the world's largest recruitment firm. Tom Johnston, who formerly advised firms on how to enter the exec temp placement market, joined Management Recruiters to develop the program last year. Today, Management Recruiters' 585 franchised offices with 3,000 recruiters nationwide are trained to provide exec temp placement. InterExec maintains a national database of candidates, DBSky, linked to all offices. Since InterExec opened in October '93, Johnston has seen a tremendous growth and placement rate (30% convert to permanent) with several hundred placements to date.

Management Recruiters/InterExec is also involved in a pilot program with a Fortune 50 company that has been downsizing. In addition to taking thousands of candidates into its database, InterExec has been working on a method to allow a company to retain an executive for say 60 percent of the time and have the exec placed in interim positions for the remainder. The "lending" company remains the employer of record in this "lending execs" outsourcing arrangement.

News & Notes

• Even the academic world now has the opportunity to employ interim execs. Thomas H. Langevin, a former college president from Mountain Home, AR, maintains the Registry of Interim College and University Presidents. When called upon for permanent placement, Langevin recommends Washington, D.C. executive search firm, R.H. Perry & Associates. Perry, in turn, sends temporary search clients to the Registry.

• The military also has a presence in the interim executive market in the person of Lt. General Vernon Kondra, USAF Ret. Lt. General Kondra directed the airlift logistics for the Gulf War. He is a principal with Douglas Reiter Co. in Portland OR. Kondra's unique knowledge and abilities have been tapped as an interim executive at IBM Federal Systems Company (now LORAL Federal Systems) to work on the Air Force Global Transportation Network Contract. Kondra is concurrently performing as an interim general manager for First Interstate Banks!

• Paul Dinte, former president and CEO of the now-closed Morgan & Banks Washington DC office, has created Dinte Resources to pursue interim executive management (40-50% of the business), retained search and outplacement work. Dinte Resources is placing 12 to 15 interim executives per month; 40% go permanent. Hot areas for Dinte are federal government contractors, hi-tech, healthcare organizations and financial institutions.

Interesting related service

In an intriguing spinoff from exec temp placement, Questor Management Resources Ltd. (Port Hamble, Satchell Lane, Hamble, Hampshire S031 4NN U.K., 011-44-70-345-7775) offers The Questor Register as a service for search and management consulting firms in the U.K. The service provides an on-line database of candidates (independent executives and consultants) available for interim executive assignments. Questor licenses firms to access the database; a $350 sign-up includes system software, 15 minutes of free search time, $1.50 per minute thereafter and a $45 charge per candidate listing pulled. The on-line database, which includes two information screens and the CV for each candidate, can be searched by sets of codes relating to experience, job function, qualifications, location and more, as well as by key word.

Questor launched The Candidate Register in May '93 in partnership with the (British) Institute of Management. This database holds the CVs of managers, technical specialists and senior executives and directors who are looking for permanent appointments. Questor currently has over 1,000 candidates between the two databases. Candidates pay $90 to be on the Questor Register or $45 to join The Candidate Register. Members of three professional organizations —The Institute of Management Consultants, the Association of Project Managers and the Institute of Management — pay a reduced rate.

Director and founder Bill Penney has seen slow growth. Thirty companies use the service, but Penney finds many potential users are shy of the technology.

Opinions divided on temps future

"As active as the temp business has been, I believe that it will undergo some dramatic scalebacks as the economy gets back to normal. If the temp firms are saddled with providing a full plate of benefits, equivalent salaries and the like, then they add a profit margin . . . what advantages can they possibly offer to those companies wishing to employ their temp workers? . . . When this parity occurs, it will be just as simple and cost-effective to hire full-timers."

— Paul Hawkinson, Editor & Publisher, *The Fordyce Letter*

"Temporary workers are here to stay. Employers won't drop them now that business is stronger. Temps give them much more flexibility. If orders turn down, temps can be let go without severance or lawsuits. Quality temps will be harder to find as the economy strengthens."

— *The Kiplinger Washington Letter*, May 27, 1994

Resources

Looking for more information on this market? Consider:

- National Association of Temporary Services, 119 South St. Asaph St., Alexandria VA 22314. Phone 703-549-6287

- Association of Temporary and Interim Executive Services, c/o Christine Little, director; 36-38 Mortimer St., London W1N 7RB, United Kingdom. Phone 011-44-71-323-4300 or fax 011-44-71-255-2878.

- Executive Grapevine directory of 70 interim manager placement and related firms in the U.K., about $36 from Executive Grapevine, 011-44-81-3184462.

- *Executive Temporaries,* a guide to placing exec temps, from Search Research Institute, P.O. Box 34343, Los Angeles CA 90034

- *The Age of Paradox* by Charles Handy, Harvard Business School Press, Boston, MA 02163. Phone 1-800-545-7685.

- *The Portable Executive* by John A. Thompson, due late 1994 from Simon & Schuster.

- *The Temp Track* by Peggy O'Connell Justice, Peterson's 1994, 609-243-9111.

Some Pros & Cons

FOR CANDIDATES

Pro:

- ▲ Income during job search
- ▲ Ability to network and fill in resume during job search
- ▲ May fit lifestyle
- ▲ May become permanent position
- ▲ Fill-in during own consulting or self-employed work

Con:

- ▼ Difficult to actively search for permanent position during temp job
- ▼ Low odds for placement
- ▼ Uncertain income
- ▼ No benefits

FOR PERMANENT SEARCH FIRMS

Pro:

- ▲ Another option to offer client, additional revenue source
- ▲ May turn into permanent placement, fee for both

Con:

- ▼ Marketing may spread resources of organization
- ▼ Client may question expense and length of time frame for permanent search in comparison to interim

FOR CORPORATE CLIENTS

Pro:

- ▲ Fast fill-in
- ▲ No need to increase permanent payroll, or pay benefits
- ▲ Can tryout candidate
- ▲ Interim exec often highly qualified and experienced, has independent viewpoint

Con:

- ▼ May be privy to sensitive information
- ▼ No long-term company loyalty
- ▼ Hard to explain status of interim exec

Firm Listings

ABS Services
(a division of Associated Bankers Search, Inc.)
6404 Wilshire Boulevard, Suite 710
Los Angeles, California 90048
(213) 655-7100
Ms. Lorraine Grant
We specialize in the temporary placement of executives, management and personnel in the mortgage banking arena

Geographical area served: Southern California

Practice breakdown:
15% Executive temporary placement
15% Executive search/recruiting
70% Traditional temporary placement

ABS Services
(a division of Associated Bankers Search, Inc.)
2700 North Main Street, Suite 506
Santa Ana, California 92701
(714) 542-8300
Ms. Honey Yates
We specialize in the temporary placement of executives, management and personnel in the mortgage banking arena

Geographical area served: Southern California

Practice breakdown:
15% Executive temporary placement
15% Executive search/recruiting
70% Traditional temporary placement

ALTCO Temporary Services
100 Menlo Park
Edison, New Jersey 08837
(908) 549-6100
Mr. Ken Altreuter
Technical and operations professionals for food, pharmaceutical and personal products companies

Geographical area served: United States

Practice breakdown:
40% Executive temporary placement
20% Executive search/recruiting
10% Management consulting
30% Traditional temporary placement

ASG Inc.
30 Myano Lane
Stamford, Connecticut 06902
(203) 356-9540
Mr. Jim Baker
MIS, pharmaceutical, market research

Geographical area served: United States

Practice breakdown:
60% Executive temporary placement
40% Executive search/recruiting

ASG Inc.
3125 Poplarwood Court
Raleigh, North Carolina 27604
(919) 954-8185
Mr. Ted Phillips
MIS, pharmaceutical, market research

Geographical area served: United States

Practice breakdown:
60% Executive temporary placement
40% Executive search/recruiting

AVcaTech Services, Inc.
5855 Monroe Street
Sylvania, Ohio 43560
(419) 882-8227
Mr. Ken Wenninger
Engineering

Geographical area served: United States

Practice breakdown:
60% Executive temporary placement
40% Technical; temporary to permanent

Account Ability Now
1149 Bridgewater Place
Grand Rapids, Michigan 49501-1149
(616) 235-1149
Ms. Julie Henderson
Accounting & data processing (computer) personnel

Geographical area served: United States, West Michigan

Practice breakdown:
10% Executive temporary placement
10% Executive search/recruiting
80% Temp/perm accounting professionals

AccountPros, Inc.
152 Bowdoin Street
Boston, Massachusetts 02108
(617) 227-1212
Mr. Andrew Goodman
Accounting, financial, banking and information systems permanent and temporary personnel

Geographical area served: United States

Practice breakdown:
65% Executive temporary placement
35% Executive search/recruiting

Accountants & Auditors Temporaries Inc.
310 Madison Avenue, Suite 603
New York, New York 10017
(212) 687-5656
Mr. Walter Murphy
Ms. Joan Margarella
Financial

Geographical area served: United States

Practice breakdown:
100% Executive temporary placement

Accountants Connection Inc.
32540 Schoolcraft Road, Suite 100
Livonia, Michigan 48150
(313) 513-7800
Mr. Michael J. LaLonde
Accounting and finance

Geographical area served: United States

Practice breakdown:
20% Executive temporary placement
20% Executive search/recruiting
60% Accounting & financial temp placement

Accountants Executive Search
535 Fifth Avenue, Suite 1200
New York, New York 10017
(212) 682-5900
Ms. Hildy R. Zonis, CPA
Accounting, finance, banking

Geographical area served: United States, Canada

Practice breakdown:
20% Executive temporary placement
80% Executive search/recruiting

Accountants On Call
Park 80 West, Plaza II
Garden State Parkway
Interstate 80, 9th Floor
Saddle Brook, New Jersey 07662
(800) 327-1117
Ms. Debbie Buchsbaum
Accounting, finance, banking - over 60 U.S. offices

Geographical area served: North America

Practice breakdown:
15% Executive temporary placement
40% Executive search/recruiting
45% Temp placement below executive level

Accountemps
(a division of Robert Half Int'l. Inc.)
2884 Sand Hill Road
Menlo Park, California 94025
(415) 854-9700
Ms. Lynn Taylor
160 offices worldwide-consult white pages for local office

Geographical area served: Worldwide

Accounting & Bookkeeping Personnel, Inc.
1702 East Highland Avenue, Suite 213
Phoenix, Arizona 85016
(602) 277-3700
Mr. Michael W. Nolan
Accounting and bookkeeping

Geographical area served: United States

Practice breakdown:
15% Executive temporary placement
50% Executive search/recruiting
35% Non-executive search

Accounting Alternatives, Inc.
35 Glenlake Parkway, Suite 550
Atlanta, Georgia 30328
(404) 671-9647
Ms. Carol Cudia
Temporary, temp to perm and permanent placement of accounting and finance professionals

Geographical area served: Metropolitan Atlanta

Practice breakdown:
30% Executive temporary placement
5% Executive search/recruiting
5% Management consulting
60% Interim placement

Accounting Partners
500 108th Avenue NE, Suite 1640
Bellevue, Washington 98004
(206) 450-1990
Mr. Ted Macauley
Accounting/finance

Geographical area served: Pacific Northwest

Practice breakdown:
50% Executive temporary placement
50% Executive search/recruiting

AdStaff Personnel, Inc.
201A Rosser Avenue
Waynesboro, Virginia 22980
(703) 943-6600
Mr. Ron W. Pharr
Technical and manufacturing professionals for chemical, textile and pharmaceutical companies

Geographical area served: Worldwide

Practice breakdown:
10% Executive temporary placement
10% Executive search/recruiting
80% Management consulting

Add-Staff, Inc.*
22600 Hall Road
Clinton Township, Michigan 48036
(313) 465-4600
Mr. Walter M. Muccino
Automotive/high tech

Geographical area served: North America

Practice breakdown:
30% Executive temporary placement
70% Technical

**Firm declined to update*

The Affiliates
(The Legal Staffing Division of Robert Half Int'l. Inc.)
1901 Avenue of the Stars, Suite 350
Los Angeles, California 90067
(310) 557-2334
Ms. Florence Kanofsky
Legal - law firms and corporate legal departments; place at all levels, management and support, with special expertise in the area of key management

Geographical area served: United States

Practice breakdown:
5% Executive temporary placement
30% Executive search/recruiting
65% Support staff

Albemarle Interim Management Services Limited
18 Great Marlborough Street
London, W1V 1AF, United Kingdom
44 71 437 3611
Mr. John Hird
All industries and functions

Geographical area served: United Kingdom and Europe

Practice breakdown:
100% Executive temporary placement

Allen & Associates
1700 East Desert Inn Road, Suite 118
Las Vegas, Nevada 89109
(702) 731-2066
Mr. Bob Allen
Finance & accounting

Geographical area served: United States

Practice breakdown:
10% Executive temporary placement
90% Executive search/recruiting

AlternaStaff
(a division of Fortune Franchise Corporation)
655 Third Avenue, 18th Floor
New York, New York 10017
(212) 697-4314
Mr. Dennis Inzinna
Manufacturing, engineering

Geographical area served: United States

Practice breakdown:
100% Executive temporary placement

American National Recruiters*
6263 Poplar Avenue, Suite 940
Memphis, Tennessee 38119
(901) 767-0216
Mr. Tom L. Townsend
Management-general

Geographical area served: United States

Practice breakdown:
15% Executive temporary placement
30% Executive search/recruiting
5% Outplacement
50% Traditional temporary placement

**Firm declined to update*

Ames Personnel Consultants Inc.*
34 Hennessey Avenue
Brunswick, Maine 04011
(207) 729-5158
Mr. Philip J. Ames
Pulp and paper, environmental and consulting (A/E) firms - all disciplines; locally all manufacturing firms

Geographical area served: United States

Practice breakdown:
10% Executive temporary placement
40% Executive search/recruiting
50% Non-executive temporary placement

**Firm declined to update*

Andcor Human Resources
600 South Highway 169, Suite 1150
Minneapolis, Minnesota 55426
(612) 546-0966
Mr. K. David Hirschey
Emerging growth companies

Geographical area served: North America

Practice breakdown:
10% Executive temporary placement
70% Executive search/recruiting
20% Management consulting

Anderson Industrial Associates, Inc.
770 Old Roswell Road, Suite B-400
Roswell, Georgia 30076
(404) 641-9278
Mr. Greg Anderson
Engineering, manufacturing, most primary industries

Geographical area served: North America

Practice breakdown:
50% Executive temporary placement
50% Executive search/recruiting

Anderson Sterling Associates*
18623 Ventura Boulevard, Suite 207
Tarzana, California 91356
(818) 996-0920
Mr. Victor Goodman
Technical

Geographical area served: United States

Practice breakdown:
50% Executive temporary placement
50% Executive search/recruiting

**Firm declined to update*

ArchiPro Temporary Agency
420 Lincoln Road, Suite 309
Miami Beach, Florida 33139
(305) 532-5722
Ms. Leslie L. Swisher
Architecture, interior design, space planning, civil engineering, auto CADD specialist

Geographical area served: United States

Practice breakdown:
30% Executive temporary placement
70% Support staff production specialist

Ascher Interim Executive Services
25 Pompton Avenue, Suite 310
Verona, New Jersey 07044
(201) 239-6116
Ms. Susan Ascher
Generalists with emphasis on human resources, finance/accounting, engineering and retail

Geographical area served: United States

Practice breakdown:
35% Executive temporary placement
65% Executive search/recruiting

Assisting Professionals, Inc.
2000 North Woodward Avenue, Suite 250
Bloomfield Hills, Michigan 48304
(810) 647-9800
Ms. Nancy Black
Ms. Sharon Carlson
Generalist

Geographical area served: Worldwide

Practice breakdown:
80% Executive temporary placement
20% Executive search/recruiting

Astro Employment
14710 East Whittier Boulevard
Whittier, California 90605
(310) 698-6771
Mr. James Groom
Chemists, geoscientists, management, small business

Geographical area served: Worldwide

Practice breakdown:
5% Executive temporary placement
45% Executive search/recruiting
50% Support staff temps

Attorneys Per Diem, Inc.
16 South Calvert Street, Suite 501
Baltimore, Maryland 21202
(410) 385-5350
Ms. Laura Black
Mr. Mark Neumann
Law firms and corporate in-house legal departments

Geographical area served: Maryland/District of Columbia

Practice breakdown:
80% Executive temporary placement
10% Executive search/recruiting
10% Outplacement

Bankers On Call
507 Fifth Avenue, Suite 601
New York, New York 10017
(212) 490-2233
Mr. Stephen Shuman
Banking personnel international & domestic

Geographical area served: New York City metro area

Practice breakdown:
100% Executive temporary placement

Barton Interim Management
Bere Barton, Bere Ferrers
Yelverton, Devon PL20 7JL
United Kingdom
44 822 840220
Mrs. Nicky Cutts
Generalists

Geographical area served: Worldwide

Practice breakdown:
40% Executive temporary placement
50% Executive search/recruiting
10% Independent directors

C. Berger & Company
327 East Gundersen Drive
Carol Stream, Illinois 60188
(708) 653-1115
Ms. Katie Bartholomew
Library directors/managers/administrators; records management; sales management

Geographical area served: United States

Practice breakdown:
30% Executive temporary placement
10% Executive search/recruiting
19% Management consulting
1% Outplacement
40% Temporary library support staff

Best & Company
1085 Commonwealth Avenue, Suite 325
Boston, Massachusetts 02215
Mr. R. J. Best
General management, sales & marketing within the wholesale & retail industries

Geographical area served: United States

Practice breakdown:
25% Executive temporary placement
75% Executive search/recruiting

Blue Ridge Associates, Inc.
One Main Street, Suite 312
Eatontown, New Jersey 07724
(908) 542-4182
Mr. Jim Booton
Technical, design, manufacturing support staff

Geographical area served: United States

Practice breakdown:
80% Executive temporary placement
20% Executive search/recruiting

Boyden International Ltd.*
24 Queen Anne's Gate
London, SW1H 9AA, United Kingdom
44 71 222 9033
Mr. Michael B. Curlewis
Executive search

Geographical area served: Worldwide

Practice breakdown:
10% Executive temporary placement
90% Executive search/recruiting

**Firm declined to update*

Business Partners, Inc.
1531 North Dale Mabry Highway, Suite 102
Lutz, Florida 33549
(813) 948-1440
Mr. Joe Johnson

Geographical area served: Worldwide

Practice breakdown:
30% Executive temporary placement
30% Executive search/recruiting
30% Management consulting
10% Education

CFO Associates, Inc.
1055 Parsippany Boulevard, Suite 501
Parsippany, New Jersey 07054
(201) 402-2005
Mr. Anthony M. Bergen
Finance-general management-turnaround management-SEC reporting; part-time member of management-public company implementations

Geographical area served: United States

Practice breakdown:
10% Executive temporary placement
90% Management consulting

CN Associates
100 Smith Ranch Road, Suite 301
San Rafael, California 94903
(415) 883-1114
Mr. Charles Nicolosi
Data/voice networks, sales/marketing/technical support

Geographical area served: United States

Practice breakdown:
30% Executive temporary placement
70% Executive search/recruiting

CT Engineering Corp.
2221 Rosecrans Avenue, Suite 131
El Segundo, California 90245
(310) 643-8333
Mr. Robert Fowler

Geographical area served: United States

Practice breakdown:
25% Executive temporary placement
5% Executive search/recruiting
1% Management consulting
69% Technical-clerical

The Caldwell Partners Interim Executives Inc.
64 Prince Arthur Avenue
Toronto, Ontario M5R 1B4, Canada
(416) 920-7702
Mr. Bob Elhart
Generalists - senior executives

Geographical area served: North America

Practice breakdown:
8% Executive temporary placement
92% Executive search/recruiting

CanMed Consultants Inc.
62 Queen Street South
Mississauga, Ontario L5M 1K4, Canada
(905) 567-1080
Dr. Marc C. Raheja
Healthcare

Geographical area served: North America

Practice breakdown:
25% Executive temporary placement
65% Executive search/recruiting
10% Management consulting

The Cantor Concern Interim Services, Inc.
330 West 58th Street, Suite 216
New York, New York 10019
(212) 333-3000
Mr. Peter Bell
Mr. Bill Cantor
Public relations, corporate communications, marketing comms., advertising copy editor and writers, audio visual writers/producers

Geographical area served: United States

Practice breakdown:
85% Executive temporary placement
15% Payroll transfer services

Career Contract Services, Inc.
Banco Popular Center, Suite 1920
Hato Rey, Puerto Rico 00918
(809) 764-5579
Mr. Rupert R. Amy
Generalist senior & middle management positions

Geographical area served: United States, Caribbean

Practice breakdown:
100% Executive temporary placement

Career Marketing Associates, Inc.
7100 East Belleview Avenue, Suite 102
Greenwood Village, Colorado 80111
(303) 779-8890
Ms. Pam Tirk
Executive placement, technical contracting, employee leasing, temporary

Geographical area served: North America

Practice breakdown:
10% Executive temporary placement
75% Executive search/recruiting
15% Contracting, employee leasing

Toby Clark Associates (TCA)
405 East 54th Street, Suite 6C
New York, New York 10022
(212) 752-5670
Ms. Toby Clark
Ms. Sharon Davis
Public relations/marketing communications and advertising

Geographical area served: United States

Practice breakdown:
20% Executive temporary placement
80% Executive search/recruiting

Complimate
150 West Iowa Avenue, Suite 203
Sunnyvale, California 94086
(408) 773-8994
Mr. Ted Doyle, CPC
Provide permanent and temporary computer professionals to MIS and software development departments

Geographical area served: United States

Practice breakdown:
43% Executive temporary placement
18% Executive search/recruiting
39% PC tech support/computer operations

ConMarke USA, Inc.
3213-151st Street SW
Lynnwood, Washington 98037-2402
(206) 743-7259
Mr. Ed Clendenning
Maritime and related industries

Geographical area served: United States

Practice breakdown:
10% Executive temporary placement
90% Engineering & administrative

Concorde Temporary Staffing, Inc.
1 North Broadway
White Plains, New York 10603
(914) 428-0700
Mr. Rich Greenwald
Ms. Anita Greenwald
Office support, banking, financial services

Geographical area served: Tri state-New York, New Jersey, Connecticut

Practice breakdown:
50%Executive temporary placement
50%Executive search/recruiting

The Consortium
One Times Square
New York, New York 10036
(212) 221-1544
Mr. Martin Blaire
Banking, investment banking, brokerage, telecommunications, pharmaceuticals, for computer technical professionals

Geographical area served: United States

Practice breakdown:
45% Executive temporary placement
50% Executive search/recruiting
5% Management consulting

Consulting Spectrum Inc.
5050 Quorum Drive, Suite 700
Dallas, Texas 75240
(214) 484-9330
Mr. William Stukey
International projects, technical data processing and engineering

Geographical area served: Worldwide

Practice breakdown:
25% Executive temporary placement
75% Management consulting

Contract Professionals
(a division of Siebrand-Wilton Associates, Inc.)
P.O. Box 2498
New York, New York 10008-2498
(212) 353-2525
Mr. J. S. Sturges
All industries, all professions except data processing and engineering; established in 1986

Geographical area served: United States

Practice breakdown:
100% Executive temporary placement

David C. Cooper Associates, Inc.
400 Perimeter Center Terrace, Suite 950
Atlanta, Georgia 30346
(404) 395-0014
Ms. Barbara L. Douglas
Accounting and finance in Atlanta area

Geographical area served: Atlanta only

Practice breakdown:
50% Executive temporary placement
50% Executive search/recruiting

Coopers & Lybrand*
76 Shoe Lane
London, EC4A 3JB, United Kingdom
44 71 212 8320
Mr. Iain Lynam
Mr. John Salmon
Senior management

Geographical area served: Worldwide

Practice breakdown:
100% Executive temporary placement

**Firm declined to update*

The Corporate Staff, Inc.
177 Bovet Road, Suite 600
San Mateo, California 94402
(415) 344-2613
Mr. Stephen T. Pickford
Generalist

Geographical area served: United States, emphasis in Western U.S.

Practice breakdown:
50% Executive temporary placement
50% Executive search/recruiting

Crispi, Wagner & Company, Inc.
420 Lexington Avenue
New York, New York 10170
(212) 687-2340
Mr. Nicholas Crispi
Banking and investment professionals

Geographical area served: Worldwide

Practice breakdown:
10% Executive temporary placement
90% Executive search/recruiting

A.B. Crown International
15017 Ventura Boulevard
Sherman Oaks, California 91403
(818) 981-4002
Mr. David L. Gaffney
Generalists-wide variety of industries served

Geographical area served: Worldwide

Practice breakdown:
10% Executive temporary placement
30% Executive search/recruiting
10% Management consulting
50% Traditional temporary placement

DC Legal Support, Inc.
1899 L Street NW, Suite 500
Washington, District of Columbia 20036
(202) 775-8059
Mr. Robert S. Hamberger, Esq.
Attorney placement on a temporary basis

Geographical area served: Washington, D.C. Metro

Practice breakdown:
100% Executive temporary placement

Charles Dahl Group
416 East Hennepin Avenue
Minneapolis, Minnesota 55414
(612) 379-5311
Mr. Charles Dahl
CEO, CIO, CFO, legal, MIS, engineering, marketing, financial

Geographical area served: United States

Practice breakdown:
25% Executive temporary placement
75% Executive search/recruiting

Dahl-Morrow International
12110 Sunset Hills Road, Suite 450
Reston, Virginia 22090
(703) 648-1594
Mr. Andy Steinem
Telcom, high tech, multimedia voice & data, government/DOD, environmental, healthcare; senior level functions including CFO, Controller, President, VP

Geographical area served: Worldwide

Practice breakdown:
40% Executive temporary placement
60% Executive search/recruiting

Dinte Resources Inc.
8300 Greensboro Drive, Suite 880
McLean, Virginia 22102
(703) 448-3300
Mr. Paul Dinte
Senior executive management; CEOs; CFOs; COOs; VPs; HR, technology executives-all industries

Geographical area served: North America

Practice breakdown:
40% Executive temporary placement
40% Executive search/recruiting
20% Outplacement

Doskow Associates
919 Third Avenue, 18th Floor
New York, New York 10022
(212) 279-6161
Ms. Penny Doskow
Finance; marketing communications, systems

Geographical area served: New York, New Jersey, Connecticut only

Practice breakdown:
60% Executive temporary placement
40% Executive search/recruiting

Dotson & Associates
412 East 55th Street, Suite 8A
New York, New York 10022
(212) 593-4274
Ms. M. Ileen Dotson
Marketing, sales, general management, internal consulting

Geographical area served: United States

Practice breakdown:
5% Executive temporary placement
80% Executive search/recruiting
5% Management consulting
10% Research support/diversity placement

Dunhill Del Caribe
Call Box 2134
San Juan, Puerto Rico 00922
(809) 782-2096
Mr. Alfred P. Roach
Manufacturing, service, temp-executive/manager, finance and banking, human resources-temporary in all categories

Geographical area served: Worldwide

Practice breakdown:
5% Executive temporary placement
30% Executive search/recruiting
5% Outplacement
60% Temporary technical staff

Dunhill International Search
59 Elm Street
New Haven, Connecticut 06510
(203) 562-0511
Mr. Donald J. Kaiser
International positions - directors, sales, marketing, human resource managers, accounting/finance, engineers, plant managers, consumer, industrial, medical and telecommunications products

Geographical area served: Worldwide

Practice breakdown:
10% Executive temporary placement
88% Executive search/recruiting
2% Outplacement

Dunhill Professional Search of Lewisville
2300 Highland Village Drive, Suite 640
Highland Village, Texas 75067
(214) 317-0608
Mr. C. Michael Dixon
Technical (engineering), mid-level management - manufacturing and healthcare professionals

Geographical area served: North America

Practice breakdown:
40% Executive temporary placement
60% Executive search/recruiting

Dynamic Systems Services, Inc.
3800 North Wilke Road, Suite 485
Arlington Heights, Illinois 60004
(708) 259-3444
Mr. Michael J. Brindise
Computer and information systems professionals

Geographical area served: Chicago & suburbs

Practice breakdown:
30% Executive temporary placement
70% Executive search/recruiting

executeam
(a division of Adow Personnel)
36 East Fourth Street, Suite 1020
Cincinnati, Ohio 45202
(513) 721-2369
Mr. Jerry Kern
Most industries and functions

Geographical area served: North America

Practice breakdown:
50% Executive temporary placement
25% Executive search/recruiting
25% Management consulting

Executive Choice, Ltd.
7621 Little Avenue, Suite 216
Charlotte, North Carolina 28226
(704) 543-0396
Mr. R. Patrick Perkins
Manufacturing: senior level specialists - all industries

Geographical area served: North America

Practice breakdown:
100% Executive temporary placement

Executive Directions
4919 Spruce Hill Drive NW
Canton, Ohio 44718
(216) 499-1001
Mr. Paul E. Richards
Mr. R. Glenn Richards
Automotive systems & components, plastic molding & assembly, resins, compounds and converting and flexible packaging & converting

Geographical area served: North America, Some Europe & Asian assignments

Practice breakdown:
2% Executive temporary placement
82% Executive search/recruiting
5% Management consulting
1% Outplacement
10% Reference checking/industry surveys

Executive Extra
(a division of St. Lawrence Int'l., Inc.)
6432 Baird Avenue
Syracuse, New York 13206
(315) 432-4588
Ms. Kathi Rodgers
Manufacturing, technical, engineering, marketing, project management

Geographical area served: Worldwide

Practice breakdown:
50% Executive temporary placement
50% Executive search/recruiting

Executive Interim Management, Inc.
(a division of Compass Group, Ltd.)
401 South Woodward Avenue, Suite 460
Birmingham, Michigan 48009-6613
(810) 647-4494
Mr. Peter M. Czamanske
Industry: automotive, manufacturing; functions: senior executive level only all disciplines

Geographical area served: Worldwide

Practice breakdown:
10% Executive temporary placement
40% Executive search/recruiting
50% Management consulting

Executive Interim Management
(a division of Egon Zehnder International)
Noordhollandstraat 71
Amsterdam, 1081 AS, The Netherlands
31 20 64 64 771
Mr. Joost van Heijningen Nanninga
Generalists with branch offices in Berlin, Brussels, Dusseldorf, Frankfurt, Hamburg, London, Melbourne, Munich, Paris, Sydney, Zurich

Practice breakdown:
100% Executive temporary placement

Executive Options, Ltd.
910 Skokie Boulevard, Suite 210
Northbrook, Illinois 60062
(708) 291-4322
Ms. Andrea Y. Meltzer
Generalists specializing in human resources, marketing and finance

Geographical area served: Chicago, Midwest

Practice breakdown:
100% Executive temporary placement

Executive Options, Ltd.
625 North Michigan Avenue
Chicago, Illinois 60611
(312) 751-5413
Ms. Kay L. Gurtin
Generalists specializing in human resources, marketing and finance

Geographical area served: Chicago, Midwest

Practice breakdown:
100% Executive temporary placement

The Executive Source
48 West 10th Street
New York, New York 10011
(212) 505-1900
Mr. Richard C. Plazza
Human resources

Geographical area served: United States

Practice breakdown:
100% Executive temporary placement

Executives Pro Tem*
575 West College Avenue, Suite 101A
Santa Rosa, California 95401
(707) 542-2172
Ms. Mary Luttrell
Generalist

Geographical area served: Northern California

Practice breakdown:
80% Executive temporary placement
20% Executive search/recruiting

**Firm declined to update*

Experience-on-Tap, Inc.
175 Strafford Avenue, Suite 1
Wayne, Pennsylvania 19087
(610) 825-7416
Mr. Philip A. Cerasoli
Generalists-all industries, all functions

Geographical area served: United States

Practice breakdown:
90% Executive temporary placement
10% Management consulting

The Experts
200 Reservoir Street
Needham, Massachusetts 02194
(617) 449-6700
Mr. John Burke
General senior management; CEO, COO, CFO, director level, asset management people

Geographical area served: East Coast

Practice breakdown:
10% Executive temporary placement
90% Management consulting

Express Personnel Services
6300 Northwest Expressway
Oklahoma City, Oklahoma 73132
(405) 840-5000
Mr. Robert A. Funk
Executive recruitment

Geographical area served: Worldwide

Practice breakdown:
15% Executive temporary placement
85% Executive search/recruiting

Fearheller & Associates, Inc.
555 Laurel Avenue, #103
San Mateo, California 94401
(415) 348-0261
Ms. Gail Fearheller
Permanent & short term staffing - healthcare, investment banking, credit & collections, insurance, etc.

Geographical area served: United States

Practice breakdown:
60% Executive temporary placement
30% Executive search/recruiting
10% Outplacement

First Choice Personnel
821 17th Street, Suite 400
Denver, Colorado 80202
(303) 297-2020
Mr. Jeff Winwood
Information systems & accounting

Geographical area served: United States

Practice breakdown:
50% Executive temporary placement
50% Executive search/recruiting

Flex Execs Management Solutions
98 West 63rd Street, Suite 389
Willowbrook, Illinois 60514
(708) 655-0563
Ms. Kris Swanson
Ms. Karen Murphy
Generalists

Geographical area served: Midwest

Practice breakdown:
95% Executive temporary placement
5% Executive search/recruiting

Flynn, Hannock, Inc.
(Interim Management Staffing & Consulting Division)
1216 Farmington Avenue
West Hartford, Connecticut 06107
(203) 521-5005
Mr. William F. Coleman
Mr. Elwin W. Hannock, III
All industry generalists

Geographical area served: United States, United Kingdom

Practice breakdown:
25% Executive temporary placement
65% Executive search/recruiting
10% Management consulting

Gene Folkerth & Associates, Inc.
970 Patriot Square Drive
Dayton, Ohio 45459-4042
(513) 291-2722
Mr. Gene Folkerth
Management for: manufacturing, engineering, human resources, materials/purchasing, quality control, environmental and operations

Geographical area served: Midwest, South & East

Practice breakdown:
5% Executive temporary placement
95% Executive search/recruiting

Fortis Corporation
2035 Lincoln Highway
Edison, New Jersey 08817
(908) 248-1600
Ms. J. M. Gregory
Executive, technical, environmental, software/hardware technology

Geographical area served: Worldwide

Practice breakdown:
25% Executive temporary placement
50% Executive search/recruiting
25% Management consulting

Stanley B. Frieze Company
45 Shore Park Road
Great Neck, New York 11023
(516) 487-1959
Mr. Stanley B. Frieze
Turnaround, crisis management, workouts

Geographical area served: Worldwide

Practice breakdown:
20% Executive temporary placement
80% Management consulting

Frylance, Inc.
(a division of The Fry Group, Inc.)
18 East 41st Street
New York, New York 10017
(212) 532-8100
Mr. John M. Fry
Public relations only

Geographical area served: Metro New York City only

Practice breakdown:
2% Executive temporary placement
96% Executive search/recruiting
2% Management consulting

Furst Pro's
P.O. Box 5863
Rockford, Illinois 61125
(815) 229-7820
Mr. Kevin Reddy
Executives/managers in accounting/systems/manufacturing/business operations/engineering/human resources - temporary or project basis

Geographical area served: United States, Northern Illinois, Southern Wisconsin

Practice breakdown:
100% Executive temporary placement

G/P Contract Staffing
1628 East Market Street
York, Pennsylvania 17403
(717) 846-0000
Ms. Sara Lee Patz
Financial, construction engineers, engineers, manufacturing, electrical mechanical, environmental I.M.S., CEOs

Geographical area served: United States

Practice breakdown:
40% Executive temporary placement
30% Executive search/recruiting
10% Management consulting
10% Outplacement
10% In-house outsourcing

GMS Consultancy Ltd.
48 High Street North
Dunstable, Bedfordshire LU6 1LA, United Kingdom
44 582 666970
Mr. Charles M. Russam
All industries and all professional disciplines

Geographical area served: Worldwide

Practice breakdown:
100% Executive temporary placement

GMS Consultancy North Ltd.
Delaunay House, Scoresby Street
Bradford, BD1 5BJ, United Kingdom
44 274 723151
Mr. John A. Kirk
All industries and all professional disciplines

Geographical area served: Worldwide

Practice breakdown:
100% Executive temporary placement

GMS Consultancy West Ltd.
Maggs House, 78 Queen's Road
Bristol, BS8 1QX, United Kingdom
44 272 266531
Mr. Michael F. Dobson
All industries and all professional disciplines

Geographical area served: Worldwide

Practice breakdown:
100% Executive temporary placement

Delores F. George
269 Hamilton Street, #1
Worcester, Massachusetts 01604
(508) 754-3451
Ms. Delores F. George, CPC
Generalist

Geographical area served: Worldwide

Practice breakdown:
5% Executive temporary placement
95% Executive search/recruiting

Gibson Arnold & Associates
550 Westcott, Suite 560
Houston, Texas 77007
(713) 869-3600
Ms. Yahne Gibson
Attorneys

Geographical area served: United States, Great Britain

Practice breakdown:
100% Executive temporary placement

Glass & Associates, Inc.
Human Resources Practice
4571 Stephen Circle NW, Suite 130
Canton, Ohio 44718
(216) 494-3252
Mr. Henry F. Meyer
Manufacturing/service industries, also retail, capital goods, automation systems, food production, distribution mining, petroleum, electronic equipment, machine tools and heavy equipment

Geographical area served: Worldwide

Practice breakdown:
50% Executive temporary placement
25% Executive search/recruiting
25% Management consulting

L. J. Gonzer Associates
1225 Raymond Boulevard
Newark, New Jersey 07102
(201) 624-5600
Mr. Arthur I. Frank
Professional and technical executives

Geographical area served: United States

Practice breakdown:
25% Executive temporary placement
50% Executive search/recruiting
25% Management consulting

The H.R. Group, Inc.
102 South Tejon, Suite 1100
Colorado Springs, Colorado 80903
(719) 578-3321
Mr. Mike Boyd
Hi-tech manufacturing, software development

Geographical area served: United States

Practice breakdown:
30% Executive temporary placement
10% Executive search/recruiting
30% Management consulting
30% Outplacement

Hemingway Personnel, Inc.*
1301 Dove Street, Suite 1070
Newport Beach, California 92660
(714) 851-1228
Mr. Arne Beruldsen
Accounting and finance

Geographical area served: Southern California

Practice breakdown:
50% Executive temporary placement
50% Executive search/recruiting

**Firm declined to update*

Hergenrather & Company
3125 Riley Road
Solvang, California 93463
(805) 686-2018
Mr. Ed Hergenrather
All functions, most all industries, primarily high technology companies

Geographical area served: United States

Practice breakdown:
10% Executive temporary placement
80% Executive search/recruiting
10% Management consulting

Hire Intellect, Inc.
1810 Water Place, Suite 240
Atlanta, Georgia 30339
(404) 850-8502
Ms. Jennifer L. Lambert
Marketing and human resources telecommunications, high tech and banking industries

Geographical area served: United States

Practice breakdown:
40% Executive temporary placement
60% Mid level management temporary placement

Hire Temps
P.O. Box 3453
Mail Stop 31
Sunnyvale, California 94088
(408) 730-0880
Ms. Maria Nicolacoudis
We are a non-profit organization, placing disabled candidates with a wide range of skills in a wide range of opportunities

Geographical area served: San Francisco Bay area

Practice breakdown:
10% Executive temporary placement
90% Light industrial/clerical

Hospitality Personnel Services
190 East Ninth Avenue, Suite 190
Denver, Colorado 80203-2736
(303) 830-6868
Ms. Donna Boss-Martin
Hospitality: hotel, resort, restaurant, catering and institutional food service

Geographical area served: North America

Practice breakdown:
5% Executive temporary placement
30% Executive search/recruiting
65% Temporary support staff

Hunt Advisory Services
21 West 38th Street
New York, New York 10018
(212) 997-2299
Mr. Alex Metz
Distribution, logistics, transportation

Geographical area served: United States

Practice breakdown:
50% Executive temporary placement
50% Executive search/recruiting

IMCOR
60 Guernsey Avenue
Stamford, Connecticut 06901
(203) 975-8000
Mr. Bruce M. Clark
We cover all industries and functions, we have exceptional experience in providing top management and functional leadership and supplying management and consulting teams

Geographical area served: North America

Practice breakdown:
60% Executive temporary placement
10% Executive search/recruiting
30% Management consulting

InterExec
101 East Park Boulevard, Suite 355
Plano, Texas 75074
(214) 424-3339
Mr. Jeff Kaye
Pharmaceutical, healthcare, I.S., transportation, construction, architecture, medical devices, food technology

Geographical area served: North America

Practice breakdown:
100% Executive temporary placement

InterExec, Professional & Executive Alternatives
(a division of Management Recruiters International Inc.)
1127 Euclid Avenue, Suite 1400
Cleveland, Ohio 44115
(216) 696-1122
Mr. Thomas Johnston
Interim executives in all industries and functions for national and international assignments; contact local Management Recruiters or Sales Consultants office

Geographical area served: North America

Practice breakdown:
100% Executive temporary placement

Interim Accounting Professionals
(an H&R Block company)
200 Pringle Avenue, Suite 325
Walnut Creek, California 94596
(510) 934-7092
Ms. Nancy Nolan
Accounting & finance

Geographical area served: United States

Practice breakdown:
50% Executive temporary placement
50% Executive search/recruiting

Interim Executive Associates
16528 Calle Pulido, Suite 101
San Diego, California 92128
(619) 487-0390
Mr. John J. Foley
Mid to senior level managers and consultants for project and executive timesharing assignments; all functions and industries

Geographical area served: North America

Practice breakdown:
100% Executive temporary placement

Interim Executives Ltd.
1999 East Marlton Pike
Cherry Hill, New Jersey 08003
(609) 424-6542
Mr. Milton Lowe
Temporary executive assignments

Geographical area served: United States

Practice breakdown:
80% Executive temporary placement
10% Executive search/recruiting
5% Management consulting
5% Outplacement

InterimManagement Solutions, Inc.
6464 South Quebec
Englewood, Colorado 80111
(303) 290-9500
Ms. Judith Geist Pugh
Telecommunications, information and entertainment distribution

Geographical area served: Worldwide

Practice breakdown:
100% Executive temporary placement

International Management Service*
14650 Lenore
Redford, Michigan 48239
(313) 255-2110
Mr. Thomas Kaucic
Purchasing and materials management; all industries

Geographical area served: Worldwide

Practice breakdown:
75% Executive temporary placement
10% Executive search/recruiting
15% Management consulting

**Firm declined to update*

International Staffing Consultants, Inc.
500 Newport Center Drive, Suite 300
Newport Beach, California 92660-7003
(714) 721-7990
Mr. James R. Gettys
Architectural, engineering and construction (A&E and E&C), chemical, refinery, energy and related firms

Geographical area served: Worldwide

Practice breakdown:
50% Executive temporary placement
50% Executive search/recruiting

JRL Executive Recruiters
2700 Rockcreek Parkway, Suite 303
North Kansas City, Missouri 64117-2519
(816) 471-4022
Mr. Larry E. Eason
Engineering, manufacturing, distribution, warehousing, data processing

Geographical area served: Worldwide

Practice breakdown:
30% Executive temporary placement
60% Executive search/recruiting
10% Management consulting

Joulé Engineering, Inc.
1245 Route 1 South
Edison, New Jersey 08837
(908) 494-6500
Mr. Michael Bellavia
All engineering categories; mechanical/electrical/chemical/civil/aerospace (long-term assignments)

Geographical area served: NJ, NY, PA, Greater Metropolitan New York area

Practice breakdown:
65% Executive temporary placement
35% Design-drafting, etc., positions

Just-In-Time Professionals, Inc.
1462 East Shipley Ferry Road
P.O. Box 6004
Kingsport, Tennessee 37663
(615) 239-8877
Mr. Jim Stewart
Manufacturing - exempt professionals

Geographical area served: United States

Practice breakdown:
100% Executive temporary placement

KABL Ability Network
(a division of Syntre Corp.)
1727 State Street
Santa Barbara, California 93101
(805) 563-2398
Mr. Brad Naegle
Top management of small companies

Geographical area served: Southern California

Practice breakdown:
60% Executive temporary placement
40% Executive search/recruiting

KPA Associates
(Borrow A Banker)
180 Broadway, Suite 501
New York, New York 10038
(212) 964-3640
Mr. Len Adams
Financial services

Geographical area served: Worldwide

Practice breakdown:
50% Executive temporary placement
40% Executive search/recruiting
10% Management consulting

KPMG Management Consulting
(strategic alliance with IMCOR, U.S.)
2300 Yonge Street
Toronto, Ontario M4P 1G2, Canada
(416) 483-4313
Mr. Doug Colling
Generalists

Geographical area served: Canada

Practice breakdown:
10% Executive temporary placement
15% Executive search/recruiting
60% Management consulting
15% Outplacement

Lisa Kalus & Associates, Inc.
26 Broadway, Suite 400
New York, New York 10004
(212) 837-7889
Ms. Lisa Kalus
Engineering, construction, facilities management, building, maintenance and some real estate

Geographical area served: New York City Metropolitan area

Practice breakdown:
40% Executive temporary placement
60% Executive search/recruiting

Klivans, Becker & Smith, Inc.
720 Hanna Building
1422 Euclid Avenue
Cleveland, Ohio 44115
(216) 621-2970
Ms. Kelley A. McClelland
We cover all industries and all fields within them - we are generalists although we do have exceptional manufacturing experience

Geographical area served: Worldwide

Practice breakdown:
30% Executive temporary placement
5% Executive search/recruiting
10% Management consulting
55% Temp-perm conversion-managers/executives

Jack B. Larsen & Associates*
334 West 8th Street
Erie, Pennsylvania 16502
(814) 459-3725
Mr. Jack B. Larsen, CPC
Manufacturing, engineering QC/QA, accounting, data processing

Geographical area served: East Coast to Midwest

Practice breakdown:
10% Executive temporary placement
70% Executive search/recruiting
20% Skilled office temps

**Firm declined to update*

The Lawsmiths, Inc.
2443 Fillmore Street, Suite 319
San Francisco, California 94115
(415) 929-1090
Mr. Robert C. Webster, Esq.
Temporary placement of attorneys: we place attorneys in temporary positions with law firms and corporate legal departments throughout the state of California (Attorneys only)

Geographical area served: California only

Practice breakdown:
100% Executive temporary placement

Lawstaf, Inc.
1201 West Peachtree Street, Suite 4830
Atlanta, Georgia 30309
(404) 872-6672
Ms. Judith A. Serio
Legal-permanent and temporary placement of attorneys; division of company places administrative and support staff to the legal profession

Geographical area served: United States

Practice breakdown:
20% Executive temporary placement
80% Executive search/recruiting

Litchfield & Willis, Inc.
3900 Essex Lane, Suite 650
Houston, Texas 77027
(713) 439-8200
Ms. Barbara H. Litchfield
Professional, management and executive contract/interim staffing; all types of positions and industries; experience includes: financial, HR, systems, environmental, engineering, marketing and product management

Geographical area served: United States

Practice breakdown:
60% Executive temporary placement
40% Executive search/recruiting

Loewenstein & Associates Staffing Services*
5847 San Felipe, Suite 1250
Houston, Texas 77057
(713) 952-1840
Mr. Ron Loewenstein
Technical sales, marketing and engineering professionals in the chemical, environmental, automation products and related industries

Geographical area served: North America

Practice breakdown:
10% Executive temporary placement
90% Executive search/recruiting

**Firm declined to update*

Lowery, Cotter & Associates
2959 Lucerne Drive SE, Suite 104
Grand Rapids, Michigan 49546
(616) 949-2252
Mr. Bruce Lowery
Top financial, operations, MIS, sales/marketing and general management; positions across most industries

Geographical area served: Midwest

Practice breakdown:
5% Executive temporary placement
40% Executive search/recruiting
50% Management consulting
5% Outplacement

**Firm declined to update*

MB, Inc.
(Interim Executive Division)
505 Fifth Avenue
New York, New York 10017
(212) 661-4937
Mr. Alan M. Levine
Marketing management, financial management, general management, sales management, consumer packaged goods & industrial manufacturers

Geographical area served: United States

Practice breakdown:
40% Executive temporary placement
50% Executive search/recruiting
10% Management consulting

Management As Needed, Inc.
2625 Butterfield Road, Suite 203N
Oak Brook, Illinois 60521
(708) 573-0910
Mr. Harry H. Meyer, Jr.

Geographical area served: North America

Practice breakdown:
65% Executive temporary placement
25% Executive search/recruiting
10% Try-outs for permanent positions

Management Assistance Group, Inc.
10 North Main Street
West Hartford, Connecticut 06107
(203) 523-0000
Mr. Jack Tracey
All disciplines and industries: managers, executives and professionals

Geographical area served: Worldwide

Practice breakdown:
100% Executive temporary placement

Management Solutions, Inc.
99 Almaden Boulevard, Suite 600
San Jose, California 95113
(408) 292-6600
Mr. Richard A. Williams
Finance, accounting and senior-level MIS program management

Geographical area served: San Francisco Bay area & Portland, Oregon

Practice breakdown:
30% Executive temporary placement
20% Executive search/recruiting
50% Exempt-level/management temp services

Marshall Consultants, Inc.
360 East 65th Street
New York, New York 10021
(212) 628-8400
Mr. Larry Marshall
Corporate communications, public relations, advertising, investor relations, marketing in every industry

Geographical area served: Worldwide

Practice breakdown:
10% Executive temporary placement
70% Executive search/recruiting
10% Management consulting
10% Outplacement

The Marshall Group
1900 East Golf Road, Suite M100
Schaumburg, Illinois 60173
(708) 330-0009
Mr. Paul Silverman
All management and professional levels; generalists

Geographical area served: United States

Practice breakdown:
32% Executive temporary placement
50% Executive search/recruiting
15% Management consulting
3% Outplacement

Maximum Management Corporation
420 Lexington Avenue, Suite 2016
New York, New York 10170
(212) 867-4646
Ms. Melissa Brophy
Ms. Nancy Shield
Human resources (junior - intermediate level) primarily Northeast, limited national clients

Geographical area served: Northeast, limited national clients

Practice breakdown:
45% Executive temporary placement
45% Executive search/recruiting
10% Management consulting

McDonald, Long & Associates, Inc.
670 White Plains Road
Scarsdale, New York 10583
(914) 723-5400
Mr. William G. Long
Generalists, with specialty in corporate financial, financial services and the Northeastern United States

Geographical area served: North America

Practice breakdown:
10% Executive temporary placement
85% Executive search/recruiting
5% Management consulting

Merit Resource Group, Inc.
5755 Oberlin Drive, Suite 208
San Diego, California 92121
(619) 450-0465
Mr. Jeffrey H. Newell
Human resources

Geographical area served: Northern California & San Diego

Practice breakdown:
50% Executive temporary placement
40% Management consulting
10% Outplacement

Merit Resource Group, Inc.
7950 Dublin Boulevard, Suite 205
Dublin, California 94568
(510) 828-4700
Mr. J. Michael Burke
Human resources

Geographical area served: North California & San Diego

Practice breakdown:
50% Executive temporary placement
40% Management consulting
10% Outplacement

Mortgage & Financial Personnel Services
17071 Ventura Boulevard, Suite 201
Encino, California 91316
(800) 443-5627
Mr. Robert Sherman
Mortgage banking

Geographical area served: North America

Practice breakdown:
15% Executive temporary placement
85% Non-executive level temporary placement

Mortgage Bankers' Consultants
2711 North Haskell Avenue, LB6
Dallas, Texas 75204
(214) 841-3100
Ms. Amy Norton
Ms. Jennifer Larson
Mortgage banking

Geographical area served: United States

Practice breakdown:
80% Executive temporary placement
20% Executive search/recruiting

Mulder & Partner Interim Management
(a division of Mulder & Partner/Amrop International)
Schleissheimer Strasse #4
80333 Munich
Germany
49 89 52 32 071
Mr. Norbert Eisenberg
Generalists

Geographical area served: Europe

Practice breakdown:
100% Executive temporary placement

NB Selection Ltd.
(affiliated with Norman Broadbent International)
54 Jermyn Street
London SW1Y 6LX
United Kingdom
44 71 493 6392
Mr. Chris Behan
Generalists

Geographical area served: United Kingdom

Practice breakdown:
95% Advertised recruitment
5% Executive temporary placement

Network Personnel
1100 North Grant Avenue
Wilmington, Delaware 19805
(302) 656-5555
Mr. Barry Schlecker
Mr. Dick Burkhard
Accounting/finance, MIS, healthcare, engineering, scientific, human resources

Geographical area served: United States

Practice breakdown:
10% Executive temporary placement
80% Executive search/recruiting
10% Staff leasing

Networking Unlimited of NH, Inc.
67 West Surry Road, P.O. Box 802
Keene, New Hampshire 03431
(603) 357-1918
Mr. Denis R. Dubois
Pharmacy

Geographical area served: United States

Practice breakdown:
40% Executive temporary placement
60% Executive search/recruiting

Newcomb-Desmond & Associates
73 Powhatton Drive
Milford, Ohio 45150
(513) 831-9522
Mr. Michael J. Desmond
Engineering, manufacturing, human resources, sales & marketing, finance & banking, data processing, manufacturing support

Geographical area served: Worldwide

Practice breakdown:
35% Executive temporary placement
50% Executive search/recruiting
10% Management consulting
5% Outplacement

The Nielsen Healthcare Group
P.O. Box 3734
St. Louis, Missouri 63122-0734
(314) 984-0910
Mr. Bruce Nielsen
Healthcare management

Geographical area served: United States

Practice breakdown:
80% Executive temporary placement
20% Executive search/recruiting

Nierman & Associates*
(a division of McGladrey & Pullen)
1699 East Woodfield Road, Suite 300
Schaumburg, Illinois 60173
(708) 517-7098
Ms. Lyndy Nierman
Human resources

Geographical area served: United States

Practice breakdown:
50% Executive temporary placement
5% Executive search/recruiting
40% Management consulting
5% Outplacement

**Firm declined to update*

Onsite Staffing Solutions
(a division of Right Services Inc.)
53 West Jackson Boulevard, Suite 1320
Chicago, Illinois 60604
(312) 939-2208
Mr. Laddie J. Polz
Human resources, finance, accounting, administrative services, all industries

Geographical area served: Midwest states

Practice breakdown:
65% Executive temporary placement
25% Executive search/recruiting
10% Management consulting

P-E International-Interim Management Services
"Park House" Wick Road
Egham, Surrey TW20 0HW
United Kingdom
44 784 434411
Mr. Nigel Corby
Broad application-industry commerce and publicsector [including local authorities and government agencies]

Geographical area served: Worldwide

Practice breakdown:
100% Executive temporary placement

PDQ Personnel Services, Inc.
5900 Wilshire Boulevard, Suite 400
Los Angeles, California 90036
(213) 938-3933
Mr. Steve Cordova
Accounting/finance, healthcare, private and not-for-profit organizations

Geographical area served: United States

Practice breakdown:
20% Executive temporary placement
5% Executive search/recruiting
10% Management consulting
65% Non-executive temporary placement

Paladin/Chicago
875 North Michigan Avenue, Suite 3218
Chicago, Illinois 60611
(312) 654-2600
Mr. Brian S. Brandt
Professionals for advertising, marketing, public relations and communications; includes creative professionals

Geographical area served: United States

Practice breakdown:
100% Executive temporary placement

Paladin/San Francisco
One Market Plaza, 41st Floor
Spear Street Tower
San Francisco, California 94105
(415) 495-0900
Mr. Christopher A. Mill
Professionals for advertising, marketing, public relations and communications; includes creative professionals

Geographical area served: United States

Practice breakdown:
100% Executive temporary placement

Parker Page Group
12550 Biscayne Boulevard, Suite 209
Miami, Florida 33181
(305) 892-2822
Mr. Harry Harfenist
Engineering, pharmaceuticals, banking, finance, hospitality, marketing

Geographical area served: United States

Practice breakdown:
30% Executive temporary placement
70% Executive search/recruiting

Part-Time Professional Placements, Inc.
9812 Falls Road, Suite 114-293
Potomac, Maryland 20854
(301) 299-7991
Ms. Diane Charness
All professionals looking for permanent part-time or temporary positions whether they be full-time or part-time

Geographical area served: Washington, DC Metropolitan area

Practice breakdown:
50% Executive temporary placement
50% Executive search

Part Time Resources
399 East Putnam Avenue
Cos Cob, Connecticut 06807
(203) 629-3255
Ms. Nadine Mockler
All

Geographical area served: New York, New Jersey, Connecticut

Practice breakdown:
50% Executive temporary placement
50% Executive search/recruiting

Praxis Executive Taskforce Ltd.
Norfolk House, The Courtyard
Gorsey Lane
Coleshill, B46 1JA, United Kingdom
44 675 466812
Mr. Carl Hague
Generalist

Geographical area served: Worldwide

Practice breakdown:
100% Executive temporary placement

Princeton Entrepreneurial Resources
P.O. Box 2051
Princeton, New Jersey 08543
(609) 243-0010
Ms. Karin B. Stratmeyer
Interim & transitional management in all industries

Geographical area served: Worldwide

Practice breakdown:
50% Executive temporary placement
50% Transitional management

Pro Tem, Professional Staffing Services
1001 SW Fifth Avenue, Suite 1225
Portland, Oregon 97204
(503) 228-1177
Ms. Jo Rymer
Sales & marketing, human resources

Geographical area served: Worldwide

Practice breakdown:
10% Executive temporary placement
90% Temporary office/technical support

ProResource, Inc.
1801 East Ninth Street
500 Ohio Savings Plaza
Cleveland, Ohio 44114
(216) 579-1515
Ms. Marilou Myrick, CPC
Generalists-finance, general management, human resources, marketing management, training, production management

Geographical area served: United States

Practice breakdown:
90% Executive temporary placement
2% Management consulting
8% Outsourcing HR services

Professional Assignments of New York, Inc.
31 East 32nd Street, Suite 300
New York, New York 10016
(212) 481-8484
Mr. Bruce Sklover
Publishing

Geographical area served: North America

Practice breakdown:
50% Executive temporary placement
50% Executive search/recruiting

Professional Balance, LC
3419 Westminster, Suite 339
Dallas, Texas 75205
(214) 349-4766
Ms. Jeanne Athos-Adler
Ms. Lucy von Buttlar
Specialize in interim full time or part time positions for executives professionals in banking, finance, accounting, human resources, marketing, marketing research, information systems, sales, etc.

Geographical area served: Dallas/Ft. Worth Metro areas

Practice breakdown:
75% Executive temporary placement
25% Executive search/recruiting

The Professional Resource Group*
2141 North Academy Boulevard
Colorado Springs, Colorado 80909
(719) 597-3360
Mr. Michael A. Boyd
General management, technical management, operations management

Geographical area served: United States

Practice breakdown:
10% Executive temporary placement
10% Executive search/recruiting
30% Management consulting
50% Outplacement

**Firm declined to update*

Professional Resources Group, Inc.
1331 50th Street, Suite 102
West Des Moines, Iowa 50266
(515) 222-0248
Mr. Tom Hildebrand
Generalists

Geographical area served: United States

Practice breakdown:
95% Executive temporary placement
5% Management consulting

Professional Staffing Resources
7077 Bonneval Road, Suite 650
Jacksonville, Florida 32216
(904) 296-7760
Ms. Kristi Exler
Legal - law firms, government, corporate legal departments; place at all levels, attorneys and support staff

Geographical area served: United States

Practice breakdown:
95% Executive temporary placement
5% Executive search/recruiting

Protem
(a division of Heidrick & Struggles)
100 Piccadilly
London, W1V 9FN, United Kingdom
44 71 355 3683
Mr. Richard Ball
Generalist

Geographical area served: Worldwide

Practice breakdown:
100% Executive temporary placement

QCI Technical Staffing
4705 Illinois Road, Suite 102
Ft. Wayne, Indiana 46804
(219) 436-9797
Mr. William E. Quackenbush
Technical, engineering, computer

Geographical area served: United States

Practice breakdown:
100% Executive temporary placement

Raniere Associates
50 Broadway, Suite 1603
New York, New York 10004
(212) 943-2121
Mr. Howell A. Johnson
Emerging markets, investment banking

Geographical area served: Worldwide

Practice breakdown:
20% Executive temporary placement
70% Executive search/recruiting
10% Management consulting

Reardon Associates
27 Cambridge Street
Burlington, Massachusetts 01803
(617) 270-4400
Ms. Michelle Kramer
Human resources, finance/accounting, MIS, manufacturing

Geographical area served: New England

Practice breakdown:
25% Executive temporary placement
25% Executive search/recruiting
50% Temp/permanent administrative placement

Reflex Services, Inc.
1910 Cochran Road, Suite 344
Manor Oak Two
Pittsburgh, Pennsylvania 15220
(412) 341-8842
Ms. Karen M. Stuart
Managers, professionals and executives for interim assignments

Geographical area served: United States

Practice breakdown:
100% Executive temporary placement

Registry for Interim College and University Presidents
Camelot Estates, Rt. 5 Box 964
Mountain Home, Arkansas 72653
(501) 424-4056
Mr. Thomas H. Langevin
Higher education

Geographical area served: North America

Practice breakdown:
100% Executive temporary placement

The Douglas Reiter Company, Inc.
1221 SW Yamhill, Suite 301A
Portland, Oregon 97205
(503) 228-6916
Mr. Vernon J. Kondra
Senior and upper middle management, all industries, domestic and international, one person or teams

Geographical area served: Worldwide

Practice breakdown:
60% Executive temporary placement
20% Executive search/recruiting
20% Management consulting

Resource Integration, Inc.
(a strategic partnership with Kurtz Pro-Search, Inc.)
P.O. Box 4263
Warren, New Jersey 07059-0263
(908) 647-7789
Mr. Sheldon I. Kurtz
Computer & telecommunications industries

Geographical area served: United States

Practice breakdown:
50% Executive temporary placement
50% Management consulting

Resource Management Services
1501 Fourth Avenue
450 Century Square
Seattle, Washington 98101
(206) 223-8991
Ms. Cynthia Cross
Accounting and finance, marketing, human resources, information technology, management consulting

Geographical area served: North America

Practice breakdown:
70% Executive temporary placement
10% Executive search/recruiting
10% Management consulting
10% Outplacement

Romac & Associates*
193 Middle Street, 3rd Floor
P.O. Box 7040
Portland, Maine 04112
(207) 773-4749
Mr. Louis LaPierre
Full service temporary and permanent; accounting, finance, banking, data processing-consult white pages for local office

Geographical area served: United States

Practice breakdown:
50% Executive temporary placement
50% Executive search/recruiting

**Firm declined to update*

Romac & Associates
1300 North Market Street, Suite 501
Wilmington, Delaware 19801
(302) 658-6181
Mr. Domenic L. Vacca
Banking, finance, accounting

Geographical area served: Delaware Valley

Practice breakdown:
10% Executive temporary placement
90% Executive search/recruiting

Romac Professional Temporaries
120 West Hyde Park Place, Suite 200
Tampa, Florida 33606
(813) 258-8855
Ms. Maureen A. Rorech
Financial & accounting temporary placement

Geographical area served: United States

Practice breakdown:
80% Executive temporary placement
20% Executive search/recruiting

Romac & Associates
3 Ravinia Drive, Suite 1460
Atlanta, Georgia 30346
(404) 604-3880
Mr. Gary Campbell
Accounting & information systems

Geographical area served: United States

Practice breakdown:
80% Executive temporary placement
20% Executive search/recruiting

Romac & Associates
125 Summer Street
Boston, Massachusetts 02110
(617) 439-4300
Mr. Brian C. Cuddy
Financial & accounting professionals
Geographical area served: New England, specifically Boston
Practice breakdown:
5% Executive temporary placement
95% Executive search/recruiting

Romac & Associates of Kansas City
911 Main Street, Suite 1700
Kansas City, Missouri 64105
(816) 221-1020
Mr. Ted Howe
Accounting, banking and finance
Geographical area served: United States
Practice breakdown:
5% Executive temporary placement
45% Executive search/recruiting
50% Professional temporary placement

Romac & Associates
1700 Market Street, Suite 2702
Philadelphia, Pennsylvania 19103
(215) 568-6810
Mr. Harry J. Sauer
Financial/accounting/banking; permanent & temporary
Geographical area served: United States
Practice breakdown:
50% Executive temporary placement
50% Executive search/recruiting

Romac & Associates
1770 Kirby Parkway, Suite 216
Memphis, Tennessee 38138
(901) 756-6050
Mr. Charles G. Haddad
Full service temporary and permanent; accounting, finance, banking
Geographical area served: United States
Practice breakdown:
70% Executive temporary placement
30% Executive search/recruiting

Romac & Associates
4350 North Fairfax Drive, Suite 510
Arlington, Virginia 22203
(703) 351-7600
Mr. John A. Voigt
Full service temporary and permanent; accounting, finance, including controllers, CFO systems consultants, CPAs, etc.
Geographical area served: United States
Practice breakdown:
30% Executive temporary placement
40% Executive search/recruiting
30% Lower level temp < $50,000

Russell Personnel - Execuscope Division
120 Montgomery Street, 3rd Floor
San Francisco, California 94104
(415) 781-1444
Ms. Rosalind N. Katz
Accounting, MIS, executive retail, general business
Geographical area served: United States
Practice breakdown:
25% Executive temporary placement
75% Executive search/recruiting

Ryan Miller Temporary Accounting Professionals (TAP)
4601 Wilshire Boulevard, Suite 225
Los Angeles, California 90010
(213) 938-4768
Ms. Chris Eberhardt
Finance, accounting, banking, corporate finance and treasury
Geographical area served: North America, Europe
Practice breakdown:
15% Executive temporary placement
85% Executive search/recruiting

Sanford Rose Associates
(SRA International, Inc.)
265 South Main Street, Suite 100
Akron, Ohio 44308
(216) 762-7162
Mr. Douglas R. Eilertson
Manufacturing, engineering, computer, financial, chemical, food, medical and professional services
Geographical area served: Worldwide
Practice breakdown:
5% Executive temporary placement
90% Executive search/recruiting
5% Management consulting

Scott-Wayne Associates, Inc.
100 Charles River Plaza, 4th Floor
Boston, Massachusetts 02114
(617) 723-7007
Mr. Christopher Smith
Accounting, banking, financial services & MIS
Geographical area served: New England
Practice breakdown:
20% Executive temporary placement
80% Executive search/recruiting

Search Consultants Int'l., Inc.
4545 Post Oak Place, Suite 208
Houston, Texas 77027
(713) 622-9188
Mr. S. Joseph Baker, CPC
Engineering & executive search-strong focus on contract environmental internationally, also active in independent power industry, as well as chemicals, oil & gas
Geographical area served: Worldwide
Practice breakdown:
40% Executive temporary placement
60% Executive search/recruiting

Senior Career Placement Service
257 Park Avenue South, 2nd Floor
New York, New York 10010
(212) 529-6660
Mr. David R. Willcox
Generalist
Geographical area served: United States
Practice breakdown:
25% Executive temporary placement
60% Executive search/recruiting
15% Management consulting

Sensible Solutions, Inc.
239 West Coolidge Avenue
Barrington, Illinois 60010
(708) 382-0070
Mr. Patrick Delaney
Generalists focused on Midwest regional requirements; we are especially comfortable with technology, sales & marketing and general management assignments

Geographical area served: Midwest regional

Practice breakdown:
60% Executive temporary placement
30% Executive search/recruiting
10% Management consulting

John Shell Associates, Inc.
115 Atrium Way, Suite 223
Columbia, South Carolina 29224
(803) 788-6619
Mr. John C. Shell, III
Accounting, finance

Geographical area served: United States

Practice breakdown:
5% Executive temporary placement
50% Executive search/recruiting
45% Accountants & bookkeepers temporary

Special Counsel®
19 West 34th Street, Suite 1018
New York, New York 10001
(212) 629-9400
Ms. Lesley M. Friedman, Esq.
Temporary attorneys nationwide and overseas

Geographical area served: Worldwide

Practice breakdown:
100% Executive temporary placement

Spectra International
6991 East Camelback, B-305
Scottsdale, Arizona 85251
(602) 481-0411
Ms. Sybil Goldberg
Food, high-tech, retail, construction, sales and marketing, management, operations, manufacturing, production, engineers, HR, finance, MIS

Geographical area served: Worldwide

Practice breakdown:
35% Executive temporary placement
65% Executive search/recruiting

Strategic Management Partners, Inc.
522 Horn Point
Annapolis, Maryland 21403
(410) 263-9100
Mr. John M. Collard
Corporate renewal, corporate directors, CEO, COO, strategic planning — defense conversion in the defense, aerospace, manufacturing, computer and
marine industries

Geographical area served: Worldwide

Practice breakdown:
20% Executive temporary placement
20% Executive search/recruiting
30% Management consulting
30% Interim management

TAD Technical Services*
14014 Ventura Boulevard, Suite 200
Sherman Oaks, California 91423
(818) 905-5955
Ms. Norma Brody
Mr. Dwight Troutman
Engineers: hardware and software; import, export; network engineer or CNE; data communications; telecommunications

Geographical area served: North America

Practice breakdown:
50% Executive temporary placement
50% Executive search/recruiting

**Firm declined to update*

TOD Inc./Staffing Services
690 Market Street, Suite 100
San Francisco, California 94104
(415) 392-0700
Ms. Pat Hardy
Administrative support, legal, accounting, MIS, customer service, sales, telemarketing, technical

Geographical area served: United States

Practice breakdown:
5% Executive temporary placement
5% Executive search/recruiting
3% Management consulting
80% Temporary & regular staff placement

TRS
P.O. Box 26147, 1 Marcus Drive
Patewood Business Center
Greenville, South Carolina 29616
(803) 297-3110
Mr. Dan Davis
We provide professional, technical and support personnel for temporary, long-term and permanent assignments. Offices throughout the U.S., Canada, Europe, Australia and Asia/Pacific

Geographical area served: Worldwide

Practice breakdown:
50% Executive temporary placement
20% Executive search/recruiting
30% Support staff

Technical Personnel of Minnesota
(a division of The Recruiting Group)
5354 Parkdale Drive, Suite 104
Minneapolis, Minnesota 55416
(612) 544-8550
Mr. Jack R. Jones
Accounting, engineering, manufacturing, management

Geographical area served: United States

Practice breakdown:
60% Executive temporary placement
40% Executive search/recruiting

Techstaff Inc.
500 Esplanade Drive, Suite 1555
Oxnard, California 93030
(805) 485-7456
Mr. Christopher Stubbs
Engineering, MIS

Geographical area served: United States

Practice breakdown:
70% Executive temporary placement
10% Executive search/recruiting
20% Office-clerical

Temporary Assets*
(a division of Protocol Search)
776 East Green Street, Suite 206
Pasadena, California 91101
(818) 449-2214
Ms. Kelly Lucas
Accounting/finance; AS400 system programmers and system management; executive management

Geographical area served: United States

Practice breakdown:
50% Executive temporary placement
50% Executive search/recruiting

Firm declined to update

Temps & Company
6263 Poplar Avenue, Suite 940
Memphis, Tennessee 38119
(901) 681-9006
Mr. Tom Townsend
Mr. Ernie Hilliard
General management

Geographical area served: Southeast

Practice breakdown:
15% Executive temporary placement
15% Executive search/recruiting
5% Management consulting
5% Outplacement
60% Traditional temporaries

Thor, Inc.
(The Peopleware[sm] Company)
4201 Wilshire Boulevard, Suite 105
Los Angeles, California 90010
(213) 932-7222
Mr. Terry Thormodsgaard
Conversion services, contract programming, systems integration, outsourcing & business alliances, accounting, PC networks, optimization desktop publishing, legal, help desk & training

Geographical area served: United States

Practice breakdown:
20% Executive temporary placement
60% Executive search/recruiting
20% Management consulting

Topaz Legal Solutions
(a division of Topaz International, Inc.)
383 Northfield Avenue
West Orange, New Jersey 07052
(201) 669-7300
Ms. Ronni L. Gaines
Mr. Stewart Michaels
Temporary attorney recruitment for law firms and corporations

Geographical area served: Worldwide

Practice breakdown:
35% Executive temporary placement
65% Executive search/recruiting

Western Human Resource Associates
316 East Flower Street
Phoenix, Arizona 85012
(602) 279-5301
Mr. Richard A. Fishel, PHR
Generalist firm serving a variety of industries and functional needs

Geographical area served: Worldwide

Practice breakdown:
15% Executive temporary placement
30% Executive search/recruiting
55% Temporary support staff

The Whitaker Companies
820 Gessner, Suite 1400
Houston, Texas 77024
(713) 465-1500
Mr. Bruce Whitaker
Data processing, engineering, healthcare, legal

Geographical area served: North America

Practice breakdown:
89% Executive temporary placement
11% Executive search/recruiting

Geographical Listing

UNITED STATES

ARIZONA

Phoenix
- Accounting & Bookkeeping Personnel, Inc.
- Western Human Resource Associates

Scottsdale
- Spectra International

ARKANSAS

Mountain Home
- Registry for Interim College & University Presidents

CALIFORNIA

Dublin
- Merit Resource Group, Inc.

El Segundo
- CT Engineering Corp.

Encino
- Mortgage & Financial Personnel Services

Los Angeles
- ABS Services
- The Affiliates
- PDQ Personnel Services, Inc.
- Ryan Miller Temporary Accounting Professionals (TAP)
- Thor, Inc.

Menlo Park
- Accountemps

Newport Beach
- Hemingway Personnel, Inc.*
- International Staffing Consultants, Inc.

Oxnard
- Techstaff Inc.

Pasadena
- Temporary Assets*

San Diego
- Interim Executive Associates
- Merit Resource Group, Inc.

San Francisco
- The Lawsmiths, Inc.
- Paladin/San Francisco
- Russell Personnel - Execuscope Division
- TOD Inc./Staffing Services

San Jose
- Management Solutions, Inc.

San Mateo
- The Corporate Staff, Inc.
- Fearheller & Associates, Inc.

San Rafael
- CN Associates

Santa Ana
- ABS Services

Santa Barbara
- KABL Ability Network

Santa Rosa
- Executives Pro Tem*

Sherman Oaks
- A.B. Crown International
- TAD Technical Services*

Solvang
- Hergenrather & Company

Sunnyvale
- Complimate
- Hire Temps

Tarzana
- Anderson Sterling Associates*

Walnut Creek
- Interim Accounting Professionals

Whittier
- Astro Employment

COLORADO

Colorado Springs
- The H.R. Group, Inc.
- The Professional Resource Group*

Denver
- First Choice Personnel
- Hospitality Personnel Services

Englewood
- InterimManagement Solutions, Inc.

Greenwood Village
- Career Marketing Associates, Inc.

CONNECTICUT

Cos Cob
- Part Time Resources

New Haven
- Dunhill International Search

Stamford
- ASG Inc.
- IMCOR

West Hartford
- Flynn, Hannock, Inc.
- Management Assistance Group, Inc.

DELAWARE

Wilmington
- Network Personnel
- Romac & Associates

DISTRICT OF COLUMBIA

Washington
DC Legal Support, Inc.

FLORIDA

Jacksonville
Professional Staffing Resources

Lutz
Business Partners, Inc.

Miami
Parker Page Group

Miami Beach
ArchiPro Temporary Agency

Tampa
Romac Professional Temporaries

GEORGIA

Atlanta
Accounting Alternatives, Inc.
David C. Cooper Associates, Inc.
Hire Intellect, Inc.
Lawstaf, Inc.
Romac & Associates

Roswell
Anderson Industrial Associates, Inc.

ILLINOIS

Arlington Heights
Dynamic Systems Services, Inc.

Barrington
Sensible Solutions, Inc.

Carol Stream
C. Berger & Company

Chicago
Executive Options, Ltd.
Onsite Staffing Solutions
Paladin/Chicago

Northbrook
Executive Options, Ltd.

Oak Brook
Management As Needed, Inc.

Rockford
Furst Pro's

Schaumburg
The Marshall Group
Nierman & Associates*

Willowbrook
Flex Execs Management Solutions

INDIANA

Ft. Wayne
QCI Technical Staffing

IOWA

West Des Moines
Professional Resources Group, Inc.

MAINE

Brunswick
Ames Personnel Consultants Inc.*

Portland
Romac & Associates*

MARYLAND

Annapolis
Strategic Management Partners, Inc.

Baltimore
Attorneys Per Diem, Inc.

Potomac
Part-Time Professional Placements, Inc.

MASSACHUSETTS

Boston
AccountPros, Inc.
Best & Company
Romac & Associates
Scott-Wayne Associates, Inc.

Burlington
Reardon Associates

Needham
The Experts

Worcester
Delores F. George

MICHIGAN

Birmingham
Executive Interim Management, Inc.

Bloomfield Hills
Assisting Professionals, Inc.

Clinton Township
Add-Staff, Inc.*

Grand Rapids
Account Ability Now
Lowery, Cotter & Associates

Livonia
Accountants Connection Inc.

Redford
International Management Service*

MINNESOTA

Minneapolis
Andcor Human Resources
Charles Dahl Group
Technical Personnel of Minnesota

MISSOURI

Kansas City
Romac & Associates of Kansas City

North Kansas City
JRL Executive Recruiters

St. Louis
The Nielsen Healthcare Group

NEVADA

Las Vegas
Allen & Associates

NEW HAMPSHIRE

Keene
Networking Unlimited of NH, Inc.

NEW JERSEY

Cherry Hill
Interim Executives Ltd.

Eatontown
Blue Ridge Associates, Inc.

Edison
ALTCO Temporary Services
Fortis Corporation
Joulé Engineering, Inc.

Newark
L. J. Gonzer Associates

Parsippany
CFO Associates, Inc.

Princeton
Princeton Entrepreneurial Resources

Saddle Brook
Accountants On Call

Verona
Ascher Interim Executive Services

Warren
Resource Integration, Inc.

West Orange
Topaz Legal Solutions

NEW YORK

Great Neck
Stanley B. Frieze Company

New York
Accountants & Auditors Temporaries Inc.
Accountants Executive Search
AlternaStaff
Bankers On Call
The Cantor Concern Interim Services, Inc.
Toby Clark Associates (TCA)
The Consortium
Contract Professionals
Crispi, Wagner & Company, Inc.
Doskow Associates
Dotson & Associates
The Executive Source
Frylance, Inc.
Hunt Advisory Services
KPA Associates
Lisa Kalus & Associates, Inc.
MB, Inc.
Marshall Consultants, Inc.
Maximum Management Corporation
Professional Assignments of New York, Inc.
Raniere Associates
Senior Career Placement Service
Special Counsel®

Scarsdale
McDonald, Long & Associates, Inc.

Syracuse
Executive Extra

White Plains
Concorde Temporary Staffing, Inc.

NORTH CAROLINA

Charlotte
Executive Choice, Ltd.

Raleigh
ASG Inc.

OHIO

Akron
Sanford Rose Associates

Canton
Executive Directions
Glass & Associates, Inc.

Cincinnati
executeam

Cleveland
InterExec, Professional & Executive Alternatives
Klivans, Becker & Smith, Inc.
ProResource, Inc.

Dayton
Gene Folkerth & Associates, Inc.

Milford
Newcomb-Desmond & Associates

Sylvania
AVcaTech Services, Inc.

OKLAHOMA

Oklahoma City
Express Personnel Services

OREGON

Portland
Pro Tem, Professional Staffing Services
The Douglas Reiter Company, Inc.

PENNSYLVANIA

Erie
Jack B. Larsen & Associates*

Philadelphia
Romac & Associates

Pittsburgh
Reflex Services, Inc.

Wayne
Experience-on-Tap, Inc.

York
G/P Contract Staffing

PUERTO RICO

Hato Rey
Career Contract Services, Inc.

San Juan
Dunhill Del Caribe

SOUTH CAROLINA

Columbia
John Shell Associates, Inc.

Greenville
TRS

TENNESSEE

Kingsport
Just-In-Time Professionals, Inc.

Memphis
American National Recruiters*
Romac & Associates
Temps & Company

TEXAS

Dallas
Consulting Spectrum Inc.
Mortgage Bankers' Consultants
Professional Balance, LC

Highland Village
Dunhill Professional Search of Lewisville

Houston
Gibson Arnold & Associates
Litchfield & Willis, Inc.
Loewenstein & Associates Staffing Services*
Search Consultants Int'l., Inc.
The Whitaker Companies

Plano
InterExec

VIRGINIA

Arlington
Romac & Associates

McLean
Dinte Resources Inc.

Reston
Dahl-Morrow International

Waynesboro
AdStaff Personnel, Inc.

WASHINGTON

Bellevue
Accounting Partners

Lynnwood
ConMarke USA, Inc.

Seattle
Resource Management Services

CANADA

ONTARIO

Mississauga
CanMed Consultants Inc.

Toronto
The Caldwell Partners Interim Executives Inc.
KPMG Management Consulting

GERMANY

Munich
Mulder & Partner Interim Management

THE NETHERLANDS

Amsterdam
Executive Interim Management

UNITED KINGDOM

Bradford
GMS Consultancy North Ltd.

Bristol
GMS Consultancy West Ltd.

Coleshill
Praxis Executive Taskforce Ltd.

London
Albemarle Interim Management Services Limited
Boyden International Ltd.*
Coopers & Lybrand*
NB Selection Ltd.
Protem

BEDFORDSHIRE

Dunstable
GMS Consultancy Ltd.

DEVON

Yelverton
Barton Interim Management

SURREY

Egham
P-E International-Interim Management Services

Specialty Listing

Generalists

Albemarle Interim Management Services Limited
American National Recruiters*
Ascher Interim Executive Services
Assisting Professionals, Inc.
Astro Employment
Barton Interim Management
Boyden International Ltd.*
The Caldwell Partners Interim Executives Inc.
Career Contract Services, Inc.
Contract Professionals
Coopers & Lybrand*
The Corporate Staff, Inc.
A.B. Crown International
Dinte Resources Inc.
executeam
Executive Interim Management, Inc.
Executive Interim Management
Executive Options, Ltd.
Executive Options, Ltd.
Executives Pro Tem*
Experience-on-Tap, Inc.
The Experts
Flex Execs Management Solutions
Flynn, Hannock, Inc.
Stanley B. Frieze Company
GMS Consultancy Ltd.
GMS Consultancy North Ltd.
GMS Consultancy West Ltd.
Delores F. George
L. J. Gonzer Associates
Hergenrather & Company
IMCOR
InterExec, Professional & Executive Alternatives
Interim Executive Associates
Interim Executives Ltd.
KABL Ability Network
KPMG Management Consulting
Klivans, Becker & Smith, Inc.
Litchfield & Willis, Inc.
Management Assistance Group, Inc.
The Marshall Group
McDonald, Long & Associates, Inc.
Mulder & Partner Interim Management
NB Selection Ltd.
Part-Time Professional Placements, Inc.
Part Time Resources
Praxis Executive Taskforce Ltd.
Princeton Entrepreneurial Resources
ProResource, Inc.
The Professional Resource Group*
Professional Resources Group, Inc.
Protem
Reflex Services, Inc.
The Douglas Reiter Company, Inc.
Senior Career Placement Service
Sensible Solutions, Inc.
Temps & Company
Western Human Resource Associates

Finance & Accounting

ABS Services
ABS Services
Account Ability Now
AccountPros, Inc.
Accountants & Auditors Temporaries Inc.
Accountants Connection Inc.
Accountants Executive Search
Accountants On Call
Accountemps
Accounting & Bookkeeping Personnel, Inc.
Accounting Alternatives, Inc.
Accounting Partners
Allen & Associates
Ascher Interim Executive Services
Bankers On Call
CFO Associates, Inc.
Concorde Temporary Staffing, Inc.
The Consortium
David C. Cooper Associates, Inc.
Crispi, Wagner & Company, Inc.
Charles Dahl Group
Doskow Associates
Dunhill Del Caribe
Dunhill International Search
Executive Options, Ltd.
Executive Options, Ltd.
Fearheller & Associates, Inc.
First Choice Personnel
Furst Pro's
G/P Contract Staffing
Hemingway Personnel, Inc.*
Interim Accounting Professionals
KPA Associates
Jack B. Larsen & Associates*
MB, Inc.
Management Solutions, Inc.
McDonald, Long & Associates, Inc.
Merit Resource Group, Inc.
Mortgage & Financial Personnel Services
Mortgage Bankers' Consultants
Newcomb-Desmond & Associates
Onsite Staffing Solutions
PDQ Personnel Services, Inc.
Parker Page Group
ProResource, Inc.
Professional Balance, LC
Raniere Associates
Reardon Associates
Resource Management Services
Romac & Associates*
Romac & Associates
Romac Professional Temporaries
Romac & Associates
Romac & Associates
Romac & Associates of Kansas City
Romac & Associates
Romac & Associates
Romac & Associates
Russell Personnel - Execuscope Division
Ryan Miller Temporary Accounting Professionals (TAP)
Sanford Rose Associates
Scott-Wayne Associates, Inc.
John Shell Associates, Inc.
Spectra International
TOD Inc./Staffing Services
Technical Personnel of Minnesota
Temporary Assets*
Thor, Inc.

Sales & Marketing
C. Berger & Company
Best & Company
CN Associates
The Cantor Concern Interim Services, Inc.
Toby Clark Associates (TCA)
Charles Dahl Group
Dotson & Associates
Dunhill International Search
Executive Extra
Executive Options, Ltd.
Executive Options, Ltd.
Frylance, Inc.
Hire Intellect, Inc.
Litchfield & Willis, Inc.
Loewenstein & Associates Staffing Services*
Lowery, Cotter & Associates
MB, Inc.
Marshall Consultants, Inc.
Merit Resource Group, Inc.
Newcomb-Desmond & Associates
Paladin/Chicago
Paladin/San Francisco
Parker Page Group
Pro Tem, Professional Staffing Services
Professional Balance, LC
Resource Management Services
Sensible Solutions, Inc.
Spectra International
TOD Inc./Staffing Services

Human Resources
Ascher Interim Executive Services
Dinte Resources Inc.
Dunhill Del Caribe
Dunhill International Search
Executive Options, Ltd.
Executive Options, Ltd.
The Executive Source
Gene Folkerth & Associates, Inc.
Furst Pro's
Hire Intellect, Inc.
Litchfield & Willis, Inc.
Maximum Management Corporation
Merit Resource Group, Inc.
Merit Resource Group, Inc.
Network Personnel
Newcomb-Desmond & Associates
Nierman & Associates*
Onsite Staffing Solutions
Pro Tem, Professional Staffing Services
ProResource, Inc.
Professional Balance, LC
Reardon Associates
Resource Management Services
Spectra International

Information Technology
ASG Inc.
ASG Inc.
Account Ability Now
AccountPros, Inc.
Business Partners, Inc.
CN Associates
Complimate
The Consortium
Consulting Spectrum Inc.
Contract Professionals
Charles Dahl Group
Dunhill International Search
Dynamic Systems Services, Inc.
First Choice Personnel
Fortis Corporation
The H.R. Group, Inc.
InterExec
InterimManagement Solutions, Inc.
JRL Executive Recruiters
Jack B. Larsen & Associates*
Lowery, Cotter & Associates
Management Solutions, Inc.
Merit Resource Group, Inc.
Newcomb-Desmond & Associates
Professional Balance, LC
QCI Technical Staffing
Reardon Associates
Resource Integration, Inc.
Resource Management Services
Romac & Associates*
Romac Professional Temporaries
Romac & Associates
Romac & Associates
Russell Personnel - Execuscope Division
Sanford Rose Associates
Scott-Wayne Associates, Inc.
Spectra International
Strategic Management Partners, Inc.
TAD Technical Services*
TOD Inc./Staffing Services
Techstaff Inc.
Temporary Assets*
Thor, Inc.
The Whitaker Companies

Engineering, Manufacturing & Technical
ALTCO Temporary Services
AVcaTech Services, Inc.
AdStaff Personnel, Inc.
Add-Staff, Inc.*
AlternaStaff
Ames Personnel Consultants Inc.*
Anderson Industrial Associates, Inc.
Anderson Sterling Associates*
ArchiPro Temporary Agency
Ascher Interim Executive Services
Astro Employment
Blue Ridge Associates, Inc.
Business Partners, Inc.
CT Engineering Corp.
Career Marketing Associates, Inc.
Consulting Spectrum Inc.
Charles Dahl Group
Dahl-Morrow International
Dunhill Del Caribe
Dunhill International Search
Dunhill Professional Search of Lewisville
Executive Choice, Ltd.
Executive Directions
Executive Extra
Executive Interim Management, Inc.
Gene Folkerth & Associates, Inc.
Furst Pro's
G/P Contract Staffing
Glass & Associates, Inc.
The H.R. Group, Inc.
Hunt Advisory Services
International Management Service*
International Staffing Consultants, Inc.
JRL Executive Recruiters
Joule Engineering, Inc.
Just-In-Time Professionals, Inc.
Lisa Kalus & Associates, Inc.
Klivans, Becker & Smith, Inc.
Jack B. Larsen & Associates*
Litchfield & Willis, Inc.
Loewenstein & Associates Staffing Services*
MB, Inc.
Newcomb-Desmond & Associates
Parker Page Group
QCI Technical Staffing
Reardon Associates
Sanford Rose Associates
Search Consultants Int'l., Inc.
Spectra International
Strategic Management Partners, Inc.
TAD Technical Services*
TOD Inc./Staffing Services
TRS
Technical Personnel of Minnesota
Techstaff Inc.
The Whitaker Companies

Transportation
ConMarke USA, Inc.
Hunt Advisory Services

Healthcare
CanMed Consultants Inc.
Dahl-Morrow International
Dunhill International Search
Dunhill Professional Search of Lewisville
Fearheller & Associates, Inc.

InterExec
The Nielsen Healthcare Group
PDQ Personnel Services, Inc.
The Whitaker Companies

Pharmaceutical
ASG Inc.
ASG Inc.
AdStaff Personnel, Inc.
The Consortium
Networking Unlimited of NH, Inc.

Hospitality
Hospitality Personnel Services

Publishing
Professional Assignments of New York, Inc.

Legal
The Affiliates
Attorneys Per Diem, Inc.
DC Legal Support, Inc.
Charles Dahl Group
Gibson Arnold & Associates
The Lawsmiths, Inc.
Lawstaf, Inc.
Professional Staffing Resources
Special Counsel®
TOD Inc./Staffing Services
Topaz Legal Solutions
The Whitaker Companies

Public Sector & Non-Profits
P-E International-Interim Management Services
PDQ Personnel Services, Inc.

Higher Education
Registry for Interim College & University Presidents

Disabled Workers
Hire Temps